Harlem:
MART 125

sic & Fashion
EXPLOSION
rlington
125
WE REPAIR & UNLOCK ALL CELL PHONES
STORE FOR RENT
BUS
ONLY

APOLLO
Cinderella
EYEBROWS
NO STANDING
Anytime
RED LOBSTER
ONLY
BUS

MAR
IDS
260-62

T 125

Published by:
Yale School of Architecture
180 York Street
New Haven, Connecticut 06511
www.architecture.yale.edu

Distributed by:
Actar D
355 Lexington Avenue, 8th Floor
New York, NY 10017
www.actar.com

This book was made possible through the Edward P. Bass Distinguished Visiting Architecture Fellowship fund of the Yale School of Architecture. It is the twelfth in a series of publications of the Bass Fellowship published through the dean's office.

Editors:
Publications Director: Nina Rappaport
Assistant Editor: Jenny Kim
Assistant Editor: Beau Rhee
Copy Editor: Cathryn Drake

Design: MGMT. design

Library of Congress Control Number: 2018955351
ISBN 978-1-945150821

Harlem: **MART 125**

Jonathan Rose, Sara Caples, and Everardo Jefferson

Yale School of Architecture/ The Edward P. Bass Distinguished Visiting Architecture Fellowship

Harlem: **MART 125**

Edward P. Bass Distinguished Visiting Architecture Fellowship

In 2003 Edward P. Bass, a 1967 graduate of Yale College who studied at the Yale School of Architecture as a member of the class of 1972, endowed this fellowship to bring property developers to the school to lead advanced studios in collaboration with design faculty. An environmentalist and developer, Bass sponsored the Biosphere 2, in Oracle, Arizona, in 1991, and is responsible for the ongoing revitalization of downtown Fort Worth, Texas, where his Sundance Square, which combines restoration with new construction, has transformed a moribund urban core into a vibrant regional center. In all of his work Bass has been guided by the conviction that architecture is a socially engaged discipline operating at the intersection of grand visions and everyday realities.

The Bass Fellowship ensures that the school curriculum recognizes the role of the property developer as an integral part of the design process. The program brings developers to Yale to work alongside educators and architecture students in the studio and situate the discussion about architecture within the wider discourse of contemporary practice. The first Bass Studio, led by Gerald Hines and Louis I. Kahn Visiting Professor Stefan Behnisch in 2005, was documented in *Poetry, Property, and Place* (2006). The following year Stuart Lipton, Saarinen Visiting Professor Sir Richard Rogers ('62), engineer Chris Wise, and architect Malcolm Smith ('97) teamed up for the second Bass Studio, documented in *Future-Proofing* (2007). *The Human City* (2008) records the Yale studio collaboration between Roger Madelin and Bishop Visiting Professor Demetri Porphyrios. *Urban Integration: Bishopsgate Goods Yard* (2009) documents the studio led by Nick Johnson and FAT Architecture; in 2010 Charles Atwood and architect David M. Schwarz's studio project was published in *Learning in Las Vegas*. The book *Urban Intersections:*

São Paulo (2011) resulted from the studio led by real estate developer Katherine Farley and architect Deborah Berke. Hong Kong developer Vincent Lo joined Saarinen Visiting Professors Paul Katz, Jamie von Klemperer, and Forth Bagley (BA '99, MArch '01), of Kohn Pedersen Fox, for the studio described in the book *Rethinking Chongquing: Mixed Use and Super Dense* (2014). Next, *Social Infrastructure: New York* (2015) features the studio led by real estate developer Douglas Durst and Bjarke Ingels, of BIG. Furthering the series, Dutch developer Isaac Kalisvaart and Yale's Alexander Garvin and Kevin Gray describe their studio in *The Marine Establissement* (2016). *A Sustainable Bodega and Hotel* (2017) brought together resort property developer John Spence, of the Karma Royal Group, and Saarinen Visiting Professors Patrick Bellew, of Atleier Ten, and Andy Bow, of Foster + Partners. *Paranoazinho: City-Making Beyond Brasilia* (2017) presents the analysis and studio led by real estate developers, Rafael Birmann and Ricardo Birmann, of São Paulo, and associate professor (adjunct) Sunil Bald.

Louis I. Kahn Visiting Assistant Professorship

The Louis I. Kahn Visiting Assistant Professorship is Yale's second endowed chair to honor Kahn. Established in 2004, the professorship brings to the school younger architects who practice and teach. Kahn inspired a generation of architects, leading them to new insights that became the basis of their independent work. Over twenty-five studios have been offered by Louis I. Kahn Visiting Assistant Professors, all which have been published in a series of books. Here the two professorships are combined to make this unique publication. With this twelfth book in the Bass series, *Harlem: Mart 125*, it is a pleasure to present the research studio led by real estate developer Jonathan Rose with the Louis I. Kahn Visiting Assistant Professors, architects Sara Caples ('74) and Everardo Jefferson ('73).

Introduction by Nina Rappaport and Jenny Kim

Harlem: Mart 125 presents the design work of MArch students in the twelfth Yale Bass Distinguished Visiting Architecture Fellowship studio, taught by Jonathan Rose, CEO of Jonathan Rose Companies, with Louis I. Kahn Visiting Assistant Professors Sara Caples and Everardo Jefferson. The book is a collection of work produced by students in the Fall 2015 semester along with interviews and conversations with the jurors, students, and professors in summer 2017. This presents unusual insight into the afterlife of a studio and analyses of the project.

The project, Mart 125, is positioned on a through-block site at the epicenter of Harlem. Opposite the renowned Apollo Theater on 125th Street, it is a city-owned parcel where many attempts have been made in the past to develop the site as a business hub. This studio presents a unique opportunity to participate in an ongoing project with Jonathan Rose Company and Harlem's Upper Manhattan Empowerment Zone (UMEZ) to propose a mixed-use project that brings cultural programs, commercial spaces, and affordable housing to this important locale. Like many districts in New York City, Harlem is a historically and culturally rich neighborhood experiencing rapid gentrification. In this time of change there is a strong desire by the community to hold on to its legacy and character while meeting the demands of a shift in population and cultural demographics.

The book begins with interviews conducted by Nina Rappaport with the visiting professors leading the studio, developer Jonathan Rose, and architects Sara Caples and Everardo Jefferson. Seen through the lens of their own work, focused primarily on serving the public sector, it is clear how they have established the priorities and objectives of the studio. The students were tasked with designing a project that responds holistically to the needs of the community while engaging the client and the constraints of zoning and building regulations. Each student proposal is presented with a project description and a series of images, plans, diagrams, and renderings that support the underlying ideas. Interspersed with these presentations are assessments by the jurors, whose expertise ranges from architecture and development to urban planning and policy.

The studio's initial research focused on zoning and building regulations related to the site, and several student projects found innovative ways to interpret the code through design solutions that pushed the boundaries. The split zoning of the site allowed for commercial and residential development, which paved the way for many creative solutions to organizing public and private programs. While some projects featured strong architectural strategies for direct movement across the site, others embedded cultural programs that introduced new forums for public engagement. Although the project was never realized with this program, the principles and ideas inspired by the studio left a meaningful impression on everyone involved.

We would like to recognize the work of the students who participated in the studio: Eunil Cho, Dov Feinmesser, Jessica Elliot, Jeanette Penniman, James Kehl, Jenny Kim, Kirk Henderson, Katherine Stege, Melody Song, and Xinyi Wang. We also extend our appreciation to copy editor Cathryn Drake and MGMT. design for their excellent work.

Overview

Developer Jonathan Rose, Edward P. Bass Distinguished Visiting Professor

Bob Stern had previously asked me to be a Bass Fellow when I was too busy or didn't have the right project. So when he called me in winter 2015 and told me that it would be his last year, I felt that I had to do it. As an additional enticement, he proposed Caples Jefferson Architects as architectural partner for the studio. I had never worked with the firm, but their practice had the perfect sensibility for the program I had in mind.

Our firm had long advised Harlem's Upper Manhattan Empowerment Zone (UMEZ) on the redevelopment of the failed Mart 125 site, located opposite the renowned Apollo Theater, on 125th Street. UMEZ and our firm had proposed a mixed-used program—a combination of affordable housing, a creative office building, and a large restaurant—but the project was stalled. It struck me that if the process of the Bass Studio could produce innovative, inspired designs by Yale graduate students, it might be a way to get the project moving again.

Sara, Everardo, and I began working on a studio plan, with Sara Caples doing most of the work and kindly accommodating my overbooked schedule. The first day at Yale was quite an eye-opener. In the morning each team presented its studio project in a competition for students. It was fascinating to see how Bob programmed this range of options with the faculty members at his disposal. The students managed the studio assignment process, and that afternoon we were off and working. I was impressed with how wonderfully the students organized themselves with e-mail lists and divided up research tasks.

However the students were not happy when I told them that the designs would have to follow New York City's zoning and building codes, and the affordable housing would have to meet Department of Housing Preservation and Development design guidelines. They protested vehemently that this would limit their creativity. I noted that after they graduate every project they design for clients would have to follow the codes and rules, so they might as well start now. I also asked them to design to a budget. The students asked if they could design noncompliant projects to show the limitations of the building codes. I agreed but noted that they could only be second designs; the first had to comply with the standards. It became clear that the design conditions every practicing architect must contend with have not been part of the usual Yale studio design process.

To advise the class on costs of construction, mechanical systems, and other elements of building projects, we invited a restaurateur and my colleagues Caroline Vary and Angela Howard to come and speak. We also had meetings with the client, UMEZ. Sara and Everardo were extraordinary teachers. They dug deeply and required discipline while inspiring freedom and guiding, suggesting, supporting, and pushing. They bridged the aspirational and the achievable. In turn the students were creative and innovative, pushing and stretching the boundaries of the codes as they explored more socially supportive ways of living and working while adhering to the regulations and the market. Although the real-life project did not proceed, the ideas it unleashed still reverberate in my thinking and hopefully will unfold in the students' future work.

Jonathan Rose, Edward P. Bass Distinguished Visiting Professor, in conversation with Nina Rappaport

Nina Rappaport How did you become interested in housing and urban design, and who were your influences?

Jonathan Rose I am very lucky; my work is a calling. I have been interested in community development since I was a small child. I absorbed a great deal from my father, Frederick Rose, who was a real estate developer, and my mother, Sandra Rose, who is deeply engaged in inner-city education. In the 1960s Philip Johnson asked my father for his thoughts on the redevelopment of New York City's Roosevelt Island. One weekend my father took me there, and as we stood among the shells of old hospitals he asked me, "What would you do with this site?" I have been trying to answer that question ever since.

NR What is the mission of Jonathan Rose Companies?

JR The mission of our company is to repair the fabric of communities. Development is a transformational act. The world is very rapidly urbanizing, and the speed with which it's happening is not in sync with the challenges of globalization, rapid population growth, income disparity, and migration. In

many parts of the world the current pattern of urbanism is destroying the Earth's ecosystems. However, the right forms of urbanism offer the best solutions to the world's ecological, economic, and social issues. Our goal is to create models of communities that solve these issues in ways that improve the health of human and natural systems and still make economic sense—because if they don't, no one will be motivated to implement them.

NR You often talk about the idea that a good business is one that does good. How do you envision profitable development in those terms?

JR I believe deeply that all businesses can aspire to make the world a better place. If Ben & Jerry's Ice Cream can use its consumer product to support Vermont farmers and inner-city bakeries, then we can all find a way to use our work to improve life. Our company's goal is to produce projects that contribute to their neighborhoods' quality of life and outperform competitors on a risk-adjusted return basis. Our projects combine advanced thinking in terms of program, environment, and culture with low risk in terms of financial structure. Our financing structures are extremely complex; the most complicated project used twenty-three sources. This complexity is necessary in the affordable-housing world. We often spend as much time on plotting the financing sources as we do designing the building. Our company has three areas of activity: building affordable and mixed-income projects, investing in the acquisition and preservation of existing affordable housing, and working with nonprofits to build civic, cultural, educational, and health-care infrastructure for cities.

NR It's interesting that your company works with cities in public-private partnerships.

JR We often partner with cities and/or other nonprofits. Together we combine the best of an entrepreneurial for-profit organization and the strengths of community or civic organizations.

NR This appproach recalls Sunnyside Gardens, developed in the 1920s by the City Housing Corporation and Phipps Houses, a nonprofit developer with which you have recently collaborated on projects such as Via Verde, in the Bronx. How do you leverage all your expertise to do these projects affordably?

OPPOSITE Denver Dry Goods Building, Denver, Colorado, 1992. Conversion and restoration of a historic building for green mixed use, including affordable and market-rate condos, and office and retail space.

OVERLEAF Winrock International, HOK Architects, Little Rock, Arkansas, 2004. Pioneering development of a green office building.

JR The affordability of a project is contingent on its financing, and any affordable-housing project built today requires some form of subsidy to make it work. For example, the average affordable-housing apartment in San Francisco now costs $750,000 per unit to develop, so it must be subsidized. Unfortunately there's no one-stop subsidy program for social housing, as there is in Europe. So we must patch together funding from multiple sources. The nonprofits typically contribute the site and program and their deep network of community relations. We bring the development skills, oversee design and construction, provide the guarantees needed to obtain financing, and often share in the predevelopment costs. Phipps Houses is a high-capacity developer capable of handling the roles we often play. In the case of Via Verde, we put together a fantastic partnership that combined our respective strengths with those of our two architecture firms, Dattner and Grimshaw.

NR As you mentioned earlier, you are focused on developing model projects that can be reproduced. Does Via Verde represent your mission to combine sustainability, affordability, and social engagement?

JR Very much, yes! Our goal is to make every project a model for the transformation we seek. Via Verde is a terrific model—it incorporates mixed-income, rental, and cooperative units—and we think this diversity is good for communities. It is very green and has a healthy mix of communal spaces, including a children's play area, an amphitheater, an orchard, community gardens, an exercise room, and a community room. Via Verde used an insulated panelized construction system, which was new for us and worked out very well. The roof gardens and orchard are sustained with captured rainwater; the central building's service electric loads are partially energized by solar panels. We placed the exercise room on the seventh floor and the community room on top of the building, connecting them both to outdoor spaces. We have duplicated many of Via Verde's ideas in a different format in Paseo Verde, a project we built with local nonprofit APM, in Philadelphia. Via Verde is vertical, whereas Paseo Verde is a series of five-story horizontal buildings. Each was the right design for its neighborhood and its social and ecological setting.

OPPOSITE TOP Highlands' Garden Village, a mixed-use, mixed income, transit-oriented development on the site of a former amusement park, 1998–2005.

OPPOSITE BOTTOM The Cooper Union Academic Building designed by Morphosis Architects, New York City, 2006.

THE COOPER UNION

NR Is there a project that provides a good example of how you work to engage New York City's public-housing design and financing? What lessons did you learn?

JR New York City's public-housing agency, NYCHA, is struggling with insufficient funds to meet its needs, so it has been experimenting with developing some of its excess land. We just finished a new model, East Harlem Center for Living and Learning at Washington Houses, a NYCHA site, where we transformed an underutilized parking lot and playground and upgraded adjacent play areas. We then developed a school project in partnership with Harlem RBI, a wonderful community-service organization that has been growing a charter school. Twenty-five percent of its seats will go to NYCHA residents. Above and adjacent to this we are building a ninety-unit affordable-housing project that gives preference for twenty-five percent of its apartments to current residents of Washington Houses who want to upgrade. The main lesson of the project is that most "towers in the park" can be enhanced in the interest of both the public housing and its surrounding community.

NR When you work in neighborhoods with strong grassroots community-development organizations, how do you get involved?

JR The projects usually start with our being invited by an existing trusted group that has been a part of a community for a long time. They articulate the needs of the population, making a partnership easy, and we get to know the leaders so we can serve existing community goals rather than impose our own. We may provide solutions that they never thought of, but they are always in response to community needs. Since we have been doing this work for many years with a positive track record, people in the community know about us, want to work with us, and are eager to be part of the project. So we are not usually greeted with the same distrust that other developers often are.

NR How does your office work on design issues and solutions? How do you engage architecture firms?

JR We prefer to work with architecture firms based in the city where we are working that have experience with the building type we hope to develop. We work with architects who share our mission and are strong green thinkers. Everyone in our company who works in development thinks like a designer because we are design managers. Our goal is to create the conditions in which our design team can create the best work.

NR When you begin a development project, how do you integrate your focus on sustainability? What are your goals beyond the LEED checklist?

JR The design begins with the formation of a "green" design team comprising architects, engineers, and other consultants. It was not always so easy to build green. I remember going to a lumberyard in 1979 and saying, "I want wood that's been responsibly harvested. Did this come from a rain forest?" The guy working there responded, "I don't know about the rain forest. I got it from my supplier." So I asked, "Where did he get it from?" and he replied, "I don't know—it's not my problem!" So I had to create my own system of green criteria, the "Ten S's of Sustainable Development," which includes site selection, developing projects that are walking distance from mass transit, and making building skin effective in terms of insulation and solar energy. We now use either LEED or the Enterprise Community Partners "Green Community Guidelines."

ABOVE Wallace Roberts Todd, Philadelphia, in partnership with APM, 2013.

OVERLEAF Via Verde, Dattner Architects, Grimshaw Architects, Bronx, New York, in partnership with Phipps Houses, 2012. 222 mixed-income residential units, 7,500 square feet of retail and community facilities, 40,000 square feet of green roofs, and open space for residents.

Harlem: **MART 125**

The buildings we do today are less environmentally bad than those we used to build, but they are not yet truly regenerative from an ecological point of view. They don't completely recycle their waste, they still use fossil fuels, and they place a burden on the environment. We hope to move from just reducing environmental impact to actually restoring the health of the ecosystems our buildings are part of.

NR How have you applied these sustainability goals to the broader concerns of urban infrastructure?

JR In 2008 I chaired New York's MTA commission on greening the city's public transit. I led a committee that deeply considered how to green infrastructure, generating a report on how to implement the resulting ideas. Unfortunately the MTA does not have the funds to

ABOVE East Harlem Center for Living and Learning, Harlem, 2015. A 143,000-square-foot mixed-use building including 89 affordable-housing units, a new K-8 Charter School, and nonprofit office space.

OPPOSITE Jonathan Rose at mid-term jury.

carry out all of the work, although many ideas in the report would reduce costs immediately. My book *The Well-Tempered City* (2016) explores how to make better infrastructure systems to increase the resilience of cities.

NR How did you choose the site and project for your Yale studio, and how will you collaborate with Caples Jefferson Architects?

JR The site for the studio is a city-owned property in Harlem, across from the Apollo Theater. We have been working on it with the Harlem Empowerment Zone for many years. The vision for the 125th Street side is a program with a large restaurant, several local offices involved in culture and media, and a screening room to serve tenants and the larger community. On the 124th Street side there will be affordable housing, for which we hope to target retired jazz musicians, and rehearsal spaces. It is a really fascinating project in a hot area of the city with a complicated mix of uses. The goal is to make it a beautiful green building. Sara Caples and Everardo Jefferson will lead the day-to-day studio process.

Sara Caples and Everardo Jefferson, Louis I. Kahn Visiting Assistant Professors

We were already signed up to teach a studio at Yale when consummate matchmaker and dean Bob Stern called and asked us to be part of the Edward P. Bass Visiting Architecture Fellowship studio with Jonathan Rose. Our first reaction was that it would be a huge opportunity for both the students and us to be working with one of New York's great clients and see how he thinks, what kind of rigor he brings to the project, and his detailed perspective. More than any other New York developer, Jonathan Rose goes deeply into creating better living conditions in the underserved communities where we perform the bulk of our work. Although we did not know Jonathan personally, we had visited several of his projects and were impressed with the respect for residents they conveyed. This was someone we really wanted to meet and work with.

We became more excited after speaking with Jonathan, who explained that the studio brief was a proposed development for Mart 125 in Harlem. We were quite familiar with the site, having already examined it for two clients. It is a singular site because it is all of the following: a potential cultural magnet right across from the Apollo Theater; a place where both culture and living occur, with zoning that dictates the division of these two programs by a central courtyard; and a through-block site facing two streets that present radically different contexts.

As we began collaborating with Jonathan on the design of the studio brief, we all agreed very quickly that it should adhere rigorously to the actual limits of the zoning and development in New York. Our understanding of most Yale studios was that formal design questions often drive the students' projects, and we wanted the students to apply their formal skills to grappling with the constraints that confront the average residential designer in the United States, especially in terms of affordable housing. The cultural program of the 125th Street portion of the project also brought to the forefront how best to create cultural production spaces that foster Harlem's vibrant African-American heritage, currently challenged by gentrification. We intentionally encouraged the students to bring their own aesthetics to a fully resolved design solution by midterm in order to give them time to redevelop aspects of their work in the second half of the semester.

These students were a particular source of joy in terms of the way they challenged the studio's constrictions and thought limitations. We were satisfied with the way each decided how to deal with the brief's provocations to create thoughtfully and skillfully developed work with fresh architectural qualities. Each student addressed the issues differently—some elaborated them principally in models and others in drawing or painting. Some students explored the formal properties of transitioning through the site, while others concentrated on urban interactions with the building's facades. Still others saw ways that sustainable-design development could activate the streets and the building interiors simultaneously. It was in dealing with these issues that the students revealed their talents, and we look forward to following their careers for many years to come.

Sara Caples and Everardo Jefferson, Louis I. Kahn Visiting Assistant Professors, in conversation with Nina Rappaport

Nina Rappaport Everardo, how did attending Yale for architecture school inform your approach to architecture?

Everardo Jefferson I went to Pratt and then taught in East Harlem under the National Teacher Corps program. When I was accepted I already understood formal principles of design, but at Yale I learned the philosophy, intellectual underpinnings, and grand traditions of architecture.

NR What was the atmosphere like and with whom did you study?

EJ It was the beginning of Post-Modernism, yet the field was still led by the second generation of the Bauhaus. I studied with King-lui Wu, from whom I learned the simplicity of making

ABOVE 10 Bouck Court Pre-K, Brooklyn, New York, 2016. Conversion of a windowless office building into a prekindergarten.

OPPOSITE Heritage Health and Housing, New York, New York, 2002. Conversion of a garage into a social-services agency.

spaces and seeing them in plans that could become sections. I also studied with John Fowler, an architect from England; Cesar Pelli, who was a motivating force; and Kent Bloomer, who taught a course in exploring form. My strongest influence was James Stirling, not because of his critique so much as the force of his personality. He created intricate compositions that were almost out of scale; we didn't quite understand them, but they had power. I still look at them.

NR Sara, how did you come to study architecture at Yale, and which professors inspired you the most?

Sara Caples I spent my first year at a different architecture school, and when Charles Moore sat in as a critic for one of my first studio presentations, I found his approach very liberating. I was instantly interested in Yale and applied a week before applications were due. I got in, and it changed my life. Although Yale was just transitioning from its men's-school past, women were never denied access to a great studio or teacher. It was ahead of many employers in that respect.

NR Everardo, and what did you do after graduating?

EJ After graduation I went to work for Mitchell Giurgola Architects until the recession hit and I got laid off. Then I worked in the Yale

construction-management department for seven years. Returning to architecture to work for Ed Barnes, I soon decided to go out on my own. It is an odd trajectory: I see it as getting off the pyramid and then trying to get back on after being greatly enriched by the construction experience.

NR How did you meet each other?

SC We were both in the first studio Cesar Pelli taught at Yale. When he was inducted as dean we came back for the dinner, and Everardo and I discovered that both of us had just broken off relationships. It was the beginning of a long flirtation. I guess we're still flirting. We did competitions and moonlighting together for years.

Louis Armstrong Education Center. Queens, New York, 2018. Museum and performance space centered on the life and work of the jazz giant.

I think the reason Everardo came back into architecture, and why we eventually started our own firm, was the stimulus of wrestling with architectural ideas. Once we started working on our own the dialogue intensified and grew with the input of our office colleagues. I think of architecture as unfinished business, which is part of its allure. Whatever your concern is, whether others think it is relevant or not, there is room to explore and enrich the work. That excitement still drives us.

NR A great deal of your early practice was focused on community buildings and projects that build community. How have you been able to devote yourselves to this mission and carry it forward?

SC At first we operated outside of people's expectations, as an office run by a black man and a white woman who were a couple. Our clients had to be open-minded, and that liberated us. We actively chose this path. Everardo's family immigrated to the South Bronx and he was educated through the New York City public school system. I'm a military service brat. So both of us came out of populist traditions of service. Back then few of our contemporaries were trying to do serious work in the tougher parts of New York's outer boroughs, and we were struck by how much cultural variety was out there.

NR How do you work with and improve the quality of life in the diverse communities your buildings serve?

EJ In our first project, a preschool for medically fragile children, we had to think about the process of treating a kid with AIDS, what the environment should be like, and how architecture can impact the teachers and the children. That is the richness of this sort of work.

Sometimes we have ten or twenty stakeholders. We figure out the layers of issues, listen to what they're saying, and parse it all out. Program issues often get confused with those of class and ethnicity. How do you bring all of that together harmoniously? That's our strong point: taking all this stuff and making it into architecture in which everyone can see his or her own image.

SC Our process is to try a lot of different schemes, iterating slowly while folding in the input of more people.

EJ Often there's something we do late in the process that brings it to fruition in a different way than expected. It's not a step-by-step process.

NR What was your focus for the Marcus Garvey Houses Community Center, one of the first of its kind in New York City?

EJ Typically architects would put up a blob there, but we decided to construct a space maker and break it up.

SC The idea behind Marcus Garvey was to reclaim the open space, a feral dog run that kept non-gang members

ABOVE Queens Theatre, Queens, New York, 2002. New performance venue and party room adjacent to Philip Johnson's World's Fair complex.

OVERLEAF Marcus Garvey Community Center, Queens, New York, 2012. A center for children and families of the public-housing complex.

away. We found that people were afraid to send their children to after-school programs because of gang activity and crossfire. So we decided to have the building divide the site up to create distinct zones for different groups and generations so that teenage gang members could no longer control it. We created transparent zones divided by bulletproof glass so people could observe the positive activities of the center and feel safe about sending their children there.

NR You're actively applying the philosophy that architects can engage in issues of equity as agents for change.

EJ We have so many tools to make beautiful spaces that solve all of these problems through the power of architecture. Delight is important in whatever we do, along with commodity and firmness. We're old-fashioned about those values.

SC We're Modernist architects employing an element of populism in response to the communities we work with. They're so tired of chaos and disorder, and the idea of beauty—their definition, not ours—is very important to them. We design cues that the general public can interpret as beautiful. As Everardo used to say, "Make it so my mother could love it."

EJ That's why we use light. My mother was Panamanian, and even if she didn't understand the texture of the wall or the space, she understood the powerful optimism of daylight. We hope that architectural cognoscenti also take pleasure from our designs. There has to be something for everyone, like in a good movie.

NR Which of your current projects is oriented most toward an investigation of the formal, tectonic, and experiential qualities in architecture?

SC All of them explore these aspects, whether they're charter schools or museums. Take the Louis Armstrong museum: it welcomes deep jazz fans from all over the world and celebrates an artist who played hot, not cool, jazz. Situated across from Armstrong's house in Corona, Queens, this new building has to respect its unassuming residential surroundings while providing a gradual sense of discovery of the place and the man. From down the street the structure curves into view with a brass canopy and an

OPPOSITE Rendering of the Africa Center, New York, New York, 2018.

OVERLEAF Weeksville Heritage Center, Brooklyn, New York, 2014. A new educational building and interpretive landscape acting as a gateway to historic houses from a rediscovered nineteenth-century freed African American community.

ABOVE Jennie Knauff Children's Center, Bronx, New York. A preschool for children with AIDS.

OPPOSITE Sara and Everardo at the final jury at Yale.

undulating curtain wall embedded with mesh. As you get closer you discover transparencies in what initially appear as shimmering material. The visceral experience of approaching and moving through the building is of paramount consideration.

EJ The sensory, culturally specific cues are an extension of the explorations we started in projects such as Weeksville Heritage Center, where African patterns occur at many scales, in two and three dimensions, and even in the shadows. The inverted golden dome of the Queens Theatre is read as celebratory by a broad range of the borough's ethnic groups. The spiraling curves of our new pavilion respond to the joyous circularity of Philip Johnson's New York State Pavilion.

NR How have you addressed design issues in terms of both social and development interests while tweaking the zoning code in a recent project?

SC Ninety-five percent of the children attending our new six-story charter school on St. Nicholas Avenue in Harlem are eligible for free lunch; twenty percent are on the autism-Asperger's spectrum. We're trying to create architectural amenities such as taller spaces and plentiful daylight, as well as areas of sensory stillness required by the special populations we're serving. We have come up with strategies for stealing light from side lot lines and manipulating opportunities within zoning and building codes. There will be twelve top-floor apartments with spectacular views to provide the financial engine for the whole deal. The goal is to work with a responsible, committed developer and find ways to enrich the neighborhood socially in an open marketplace—and succeeding.

NR How did similar aims inform the program and site for your Yale design studio?

SC The Mart 125 studio site is in central Harlem, on 125th Street, right across from the Apollo Theater. It's a dynamic neighborhood that is rapidly gentrifying. Nostalgia for its former funkiness is a big issue for design projects in Harlem.

EJ Harlem has a compelling cultural myth—Duke Ellington lived there—but few markers remain. Gentrification is taking over, but we have to leave signs of the past. The challenge for the students was to address both the history and the possible futures.

Yale Studio

Introducing the Studio
Robert A. M. Stern, former dean of the Yale School of Architecture, and Kenneth J. Knuckles, CEO of UMEZ, in conversation with writer Colette Taber

Synopsis

Robert A. M. Stern and Kenneth J. Knuckles met at the offices of Robert A. M. Stern Architects to share their experiences serving on the studio midterm and final juries. As President and CEO of the local development corporation Upper Manhattan Empowerment Zone (UMEZ), Knuckles functioned as the client for the Yale Bass Studio project in partnership with the Jonathan Rose Companies, which acted as development adviser.

Colette Taber How would you define the goals of the Yale Bass Visiting Fellowship?

Robert A. M. Stern The idea of the studio is to bring someone from the development community to the school. Jonathan Rose is the first Bass Visiting Professor who comes from the side of development that can be called socially responsible or community based—or more specifically, community connected. By inviting him I was interested in seeing whether the students could discipline their sometimes-exuberant sense of self-expression to address the restrictions of a program with a tough, prominent site as well as all the constraints that come with building in a city like New York. I was delighted that almost all of them, maybe all of them, met the challenge with enthusiasm. The experience confirmed for me that you don't have to design completely outside the box to do something original, fresh, and sensitive.

Kenneth J. Knuckles For more than two decades this small commercial site, the last city-owned parcel on central 125th Street, had no potential other than becoming a sneaker store, and we thought there were enough of those. So UMEZ endeavored to create a special space for nonprofit artistic groups. What inspired me about the process was that these young students so quickly embraced not only the particular mission of the project and its parcel of land but also the charge of embodying the history of Harlem. The site is right across the street from the Apollo Theater, and many proposals incorporated reflections of its facade and marquee.

Ken Knuckles speaking at the midterm jury to the students, Jonathan Rose, and Bob Stern.

RAMS It's not just that the Apollo is across the street, but the students really sensed that the theater was the progenitor for this project.

KK Exactly!

RAMS This location was a mecca!

KK The students produced varied solutions, from the impractical to the inspired and quite possible. In each and every case they put their hearts and souls into the project.

CT What did you focus on in discussing the project with students?

RAMS The students' responses were quite broad, and sometimes they didn't have much connection to what might be possible. In architecture school we are always trying to nurture people's creativity and put them on a good track to move forward. We want them to recognize that architecture is a social art, and it's not necessarily about self-expression. We're not painters working on canvases that will hang in a gallery or museum, or if nobody is interested, will be kept in Grandma's attic. Buildings have to be realized in the public realm, and there is no more sensitive site in the last seventy-five years than central Harlem and 125th Street. With the Apollo across the street, the project was at the epicenter of sensitivity.

KK Yes, the context was very important. Harlem is in transition, and there are many new residents, racially and economically speaking. So this is a challenging time. There has been quite a big change in Harlem over the past two decades—many believe for the better and others do not. UMEZ has been involved from an economic-development standpoint. We asked for a spatial solution, but the project symbolized so much more. The students understood that it would have to be a

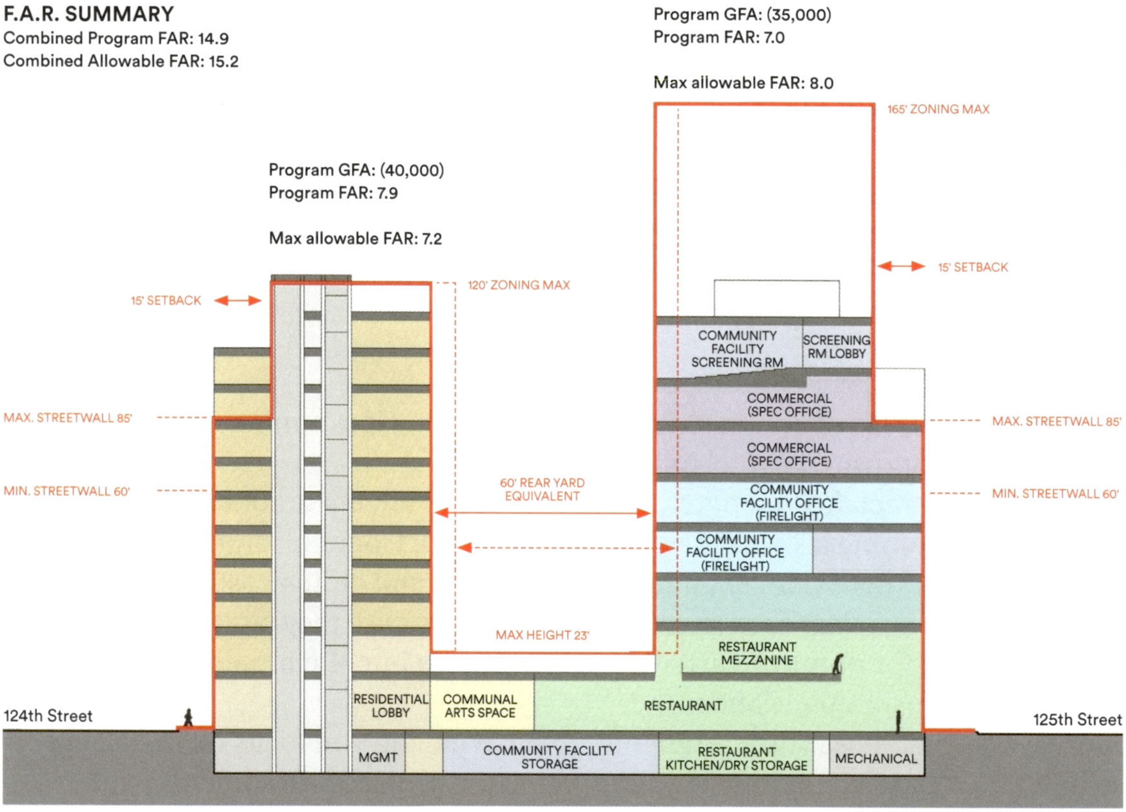

contextual project, and they addressed it in the context of their own individual expressions.

RAMS Also consider the program: first of all, the site goes through the block, which is very interesting because 125th is a wide street, with the Apollo and commercial uses, many of which are being reinvented, and 124th is a service street.

KK Exactly, a back door.

RAMS With so many commercial buildings, 124th Street was never a desirable residential street, and it is a sneaky route to the Triborough Bridge. So how do you balance the two streets? The idea of the advanced studio brief—to make music in the building and support aging musicians—struck a lot of chords, both urban and social,

ZONING ENVELOPE: C6-3 + RESIDENTIAL C4-4D
Reflects height, setback, and streetwall requirements in the 125th special district.

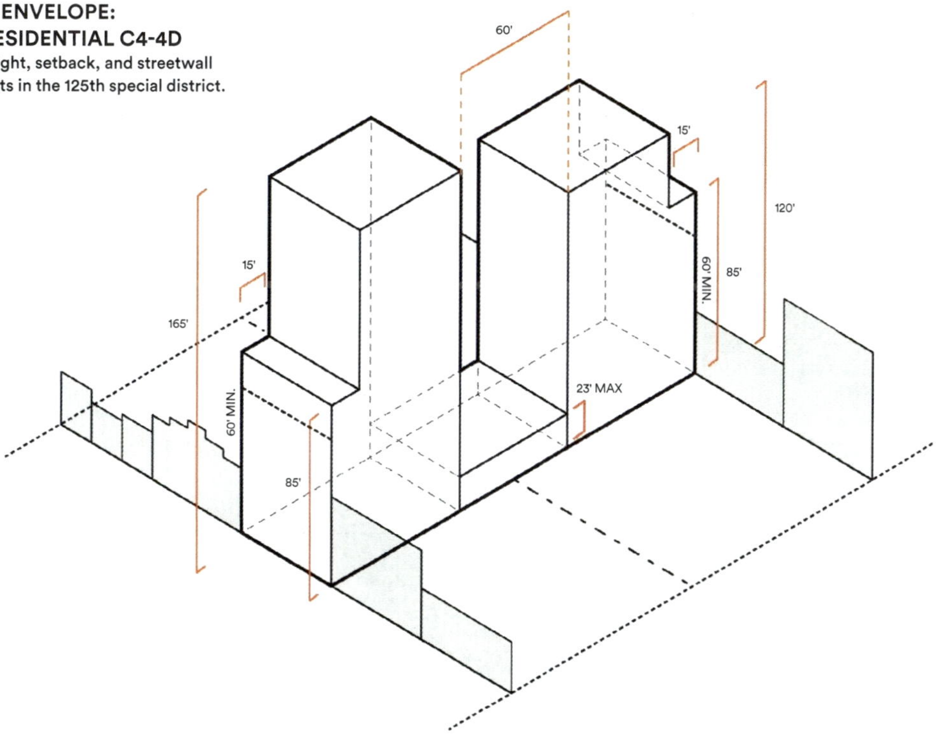

OPPOSITE Zoning envelope overlaid on program "envelope" provided by Jonathan Rose Companies.

ABOVE 3-D diagram of zoning envelope and program.

OVERLEAF The Mart 125 site faces the Apollo Theater, a legendary Harlem institution.

spot
High
Rollers
JEWELRY
Via di
La Scala
UGG
MART 125

APOLLO
APOLLO
PORTABE

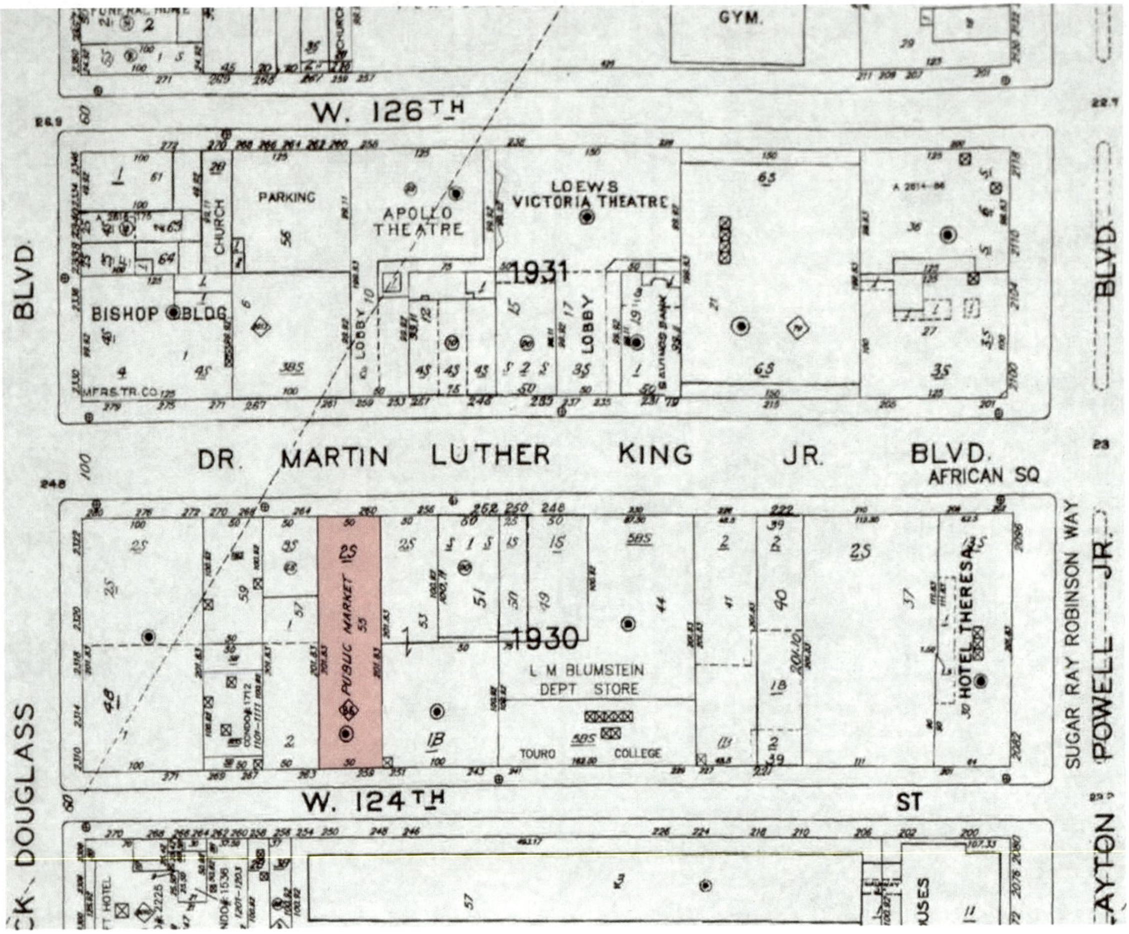

without getting into the knee-jerk stuff we often see in schools (and in real life) and without clichés about pretending that we know what people think and what is good for people. The solutions were simple and straightforward. All of the students exhibited great dignity in making the designs.

KK I agree. Each student made a personal statement, which is what architects do. Historically the back door for 125th Street's retail, 124th Street was to contain housing for jazz artists. In contrast, the 125th Street building was to host artistic groups and a ground-floor restaurant to engage street life. The building solutions were interesting and so were the spaces between the two buildings and the highly engaged way they all interacted. I think the students must have been very enthusiastic about their work. I remember when I was in architecture school long ago being given assignments that I wasn't so enthusiastic about.

RAMS Jonathan Rose was very good about framing the whole thing and getting the students to meet with his people and Danny Meyer, the restaurateur, which provided a connection to the real world. It is an experience they can take with them moving forward in their careers. Most architecture schools do not prepare students for the real world.

CT The students' solutions for the building envelope were similar, which implies set boundaries. Would you have liked to see proposals that challenged project constraints in more substantial ways?

RAMS The way you challenge boundaries is not by being a freakish person with piercings in your nose and hair worn in some bizarre way. Subtlety is a much more interesting way to challenge boundaries.

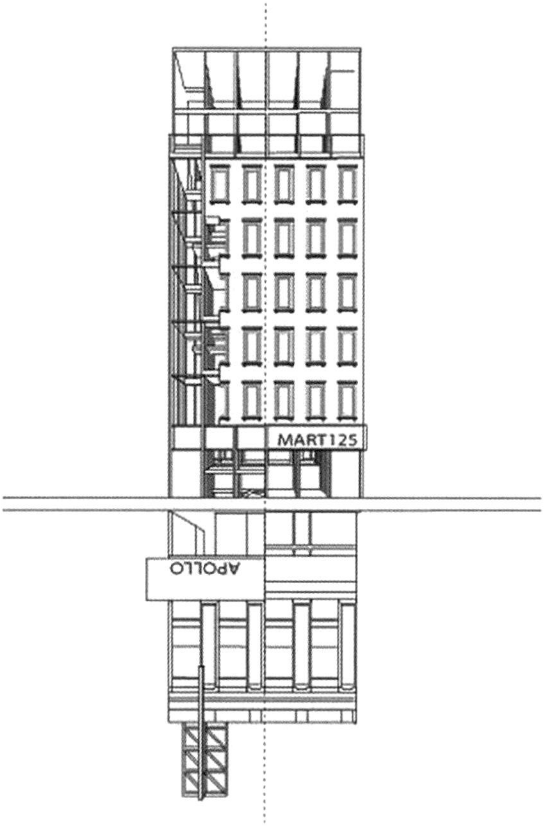

ABOVE Mart 125/Apollo elevation

OPPOSITE Sanborn map fof the site. The Mart 125 site between 125th and 124th Streets

KK The program involved a highly constrained site—an infill project, which by definition is constrained. I think the challenge was to stay within those boundaries, not just the physical limits but also those conjured by the context. The final solution had to be a departure that did not ignore the identity of the larger community, and the students met this challenge.

RAMS And they met it very well. The character of 125th Street is not embodied in a uniform architectural identity, so there was plenty of wiggle room for alternate solutions.

CT Did the students push sufficiently against development constrictions or did they focus predominantly on the immediate challenges inherent to construction in contemporary New York?

RAMS We live in the present. Things evolve, and it is hard to know what will happen next. But one thing that I can

Rendering of facade using contextual materials on 124th St. Project by Eunil Cho.

Harlem
KIDS
GAP
Factory Store

pretty much guarantee is that there will be more rules in the future. Certainly major cities will continue to experience the constraints of preservation related to buildings and neighborhood character. Harlem is a battleground, or rather a playing field, for such constraints. For instance, affluent African Americans may not want to live in Harlem any more and may prefer to live in the suburbs. How can we bring people back to Harlem? My parents' and grandparents' generations experienced something similar. My mother couldn't have imagined Manhattan's Lower East Side as a hot real estate market. "We all wanted to get out," she'd say. So students have to realize that they will always work in an evolving context.

KK I don't know how aware the students were of the larger constraints. I think they were more focused on design expression. Reality would have inevitably met whatever they proposed, but I didn't get the feeling they felt fettered by any sense of limitation.

RAMS Although I wasn't privy to conversations in the studios, I'm not sure how the students could have worked on this project with Jonathan and the others without being aware of the larger context. But when the rubber hits the road, as we both know, you have to produce a design capable of capturing the public imagination.

CT Yale tradition downplays a singular approach to architecture; ideally we want to teach students how to think as architects. How successful was the Bass Studio in this respect?

RAMS The studio was not just about Jonathan and what he did. It's also about Sara Caples and Everardo Jefferson, both Yale graduates with distinguished independent and collaborative careers. Their roles in the studio involved inspiring the students and then restraining them: like riding a horse, you have to get the horse to go fast initially and then slow down to a reasonable rhythm to prevent falling off. Sara and Everardo did an amazing job in this respect. The trajectory of their careers and work as architects is also important, and I'm sure the students were inspired by it. In fact the model presented by their partnership was perhaps more important than anything else addressed in the studio in terms of the students considering how to conduct their own careers. This is why we bring visiting critics to Yale. It's one of the great strengths of the studios as well as the seminars: students see the struggles and achievements of distinguished practicing

OPPOSITE Night rendering of facade on 125th St. Project by Katherine Stege.

architects. Many schools employ only academic architects who teach precious little connected to the real world. Architecture is still a practice.

CT Can you comment on the varied schemes in the different approaches to the building envelope?

KK The Yale Bass Studio students are from different regions in the United States and countries throughout the world, which was reflected in their varied approaches. The most interesting, and arguably the most reflective, for instance, was this one, in terms of building materials sourced in the immediate neighborhood.

RAMS The student also made some good adjustments to the 124th Street side.

KK There were approaches that represented a clear departure from the surrounding context, and it was a luxury to have such a broad and varied palette to consider.

CT How successful and inventive were the students in resolving the complications of combining a residential building on 124th Street with a cultural and commercial building on 125th Street?

RAMS The students came up with inventive visual expressions—one character for 125th and another for 124th—while tackling the divergent zoning requirements for the two streets. In essence the project boiled down to being about two buildings and how to integrate a public restaurant with private spaces for musicians. How do you bring the public in just enough but not too much? How do you maintain the privacy of the residents? The students tackled an awful lot very well.

KK This is one example of the students recognizing the kindred natures of the two buildings. They are quite different in terms of use but similar in terms of mission and users.

RAMS How they handled the street level was crucial for the success of the whole enterprise.

KK I saw many different expressions within a pretty consistent theme.

CT Jonathan Rose stated that his mission is to repair the fabric of cities, towns, and communities while preserving the surrounding land. What do you think the role of a developer should be?

RAMS Jonathan is a pretty idealistic guy, and he is the first developer

OPPOSITE Concept collage representing cultural uses and history on 125th Street Facade. Image by Jenny Kim

MA
RT 125
YAL'O

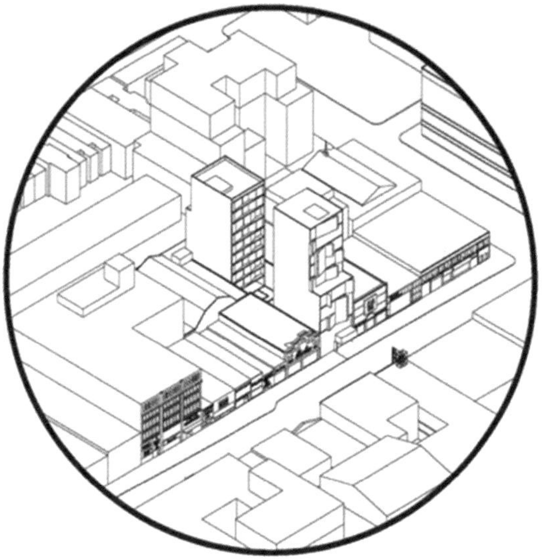

ABOVE Example of a street entrance from 125th Street by Jenny Kim.

with a community-oriented practice that we've brought to Yale. He's not a community-based developer; he's a community-oriented developer. Of course we want to see the development industry do its best to foster a sense of community. But even Jonathan, for all his idealism, has a bottom line. We emphasize this fact to students. Even nonprofits have a bottom line; you can't build on air. That's a good message for students and not one that they always get. Some students think that if the building is brilliant the money will come, which is a "field of dreams" kind of approach. I think the Bass Studio students were persuaded by the fact that the field of dreams needs to be integrated with the field of money.

KK In this case the developer's role and mission had everything to do with the history of the parcel, a place once called Mart 125. In the 1990s the city-owned building was used as an indoor market for former street vendors. Ultimately that solution didn't work, for many reasons. Nonetheless, since then the local community has viewed the site as a failed opportunity. The primary reason we envisioned a cultural use was to gain community support through facilitating public use and accessibility. The new buildings would hopefully reinforce community identity and priorities such as art, culture, and housing for artists and seniors. The development was to manifest values held dear by the Harlem community.

CT What do you imagine to be an ideal partnership between professor and student?

RAMS Bringing the student's ideas forward is an important aspect of what a professor should do when reviewing his or her work. However, every now and then—and I know I'm being politically incorrect here—the professor should tell a student that they are going the wrong way. The professor's work can also be about steering a student in a new direction. This is what happens in my professional office. People bring a project to me for periodic reviews.

Sometimes I say that the work is great and "keep going." And sometimes I say, "Uh-oh. We need to change direction." Some young students need to be told "no" as much as "yes."

KK I was a student a long time ago. I think the best thing a student can hear from a professor—particularly an architecture professor—is the truth. And even if it is an indelicate truth, I think ultimately the student is better off for it.

RAMS Very well said!

CT What are the most important trends in architecture for which the school should prepare students?

RAMS During the last fifteen or so years the digital revolution has had a transformative effect on how architecture is technically produced—but also how many architects approach design. Some architects think the computer is in charge. I still believe the individual designer is in charge of the design process and the computer is a tool.

KK To be the subject of a design studio at Yale was a great honor for UMEZ. The morning of the final review Jonathan told me to be early because Dean Bob Stern would be there only for half an hour. The dean spent half a day with us, which indicated to me that this design mission has resonance. I will always be grateful to Bob and to the students as well as to Jonathan and Everardo and Sara for the time they put into this effort.

RAMS There's another reason why I think this project was pretty successful. Usually when I'm on a review I have to go up to a student and ask, "I've been looking at your drawings, madam or sir: Where is the front door?" The student will look like a deer caught in headlights. And of course they make a lot of fun of me: "Here comes Bob Stern, and he's going to ask where the front door is." The front door is a symbol for the interface between the public and private realms of a building. And this time I think most of the students, if not all of them, addressed this key issue very, very well.

Studio Brief and Research

HOTEL THERESA
125
ST
APOLLO

The following describes the studio brief along with a detailed program and schedule that was frequently updated throughout the semester.

"Projects are not objects; they are the realization of a mission and purpose." —Jonathan Rose

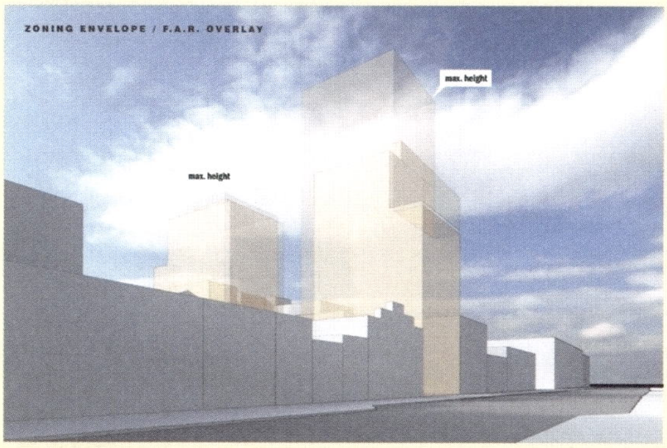

The studio task was to design a new building across from the Apollo Theater, on 125th Street in Harlem, as housing for retired jazz musicians and cultural and creative workspaces, including offices for three or four nonprofit media groups, a film screening room, a public meeting room, a restaurant/café and a visitors' desk for the 125th Street Harlem cultural district. The students were asked to question issues of cultural representation versus the mutability of the site's ethnic anchoring, especially given the distinctive qualities of optimism and tragedy in Harlem's famed cultural past. The studio required the students to consider each space from the perspective of its potential occupants. It demanded high standards of sustainable design, toward net zero, to support a more satisfying occupant experience with maximal use of controlled daylight and natural ventilation. Because innovation often comes from digging into areas that others perform perfunctorily, each project was required to demonstrate deeper consideration of the following: programming beyond defining spatial sizes and arrangements; building construction involving all major building systems and detailed sustainable envelope construction; cultural issues and their possible impact on the physical construction and the visitors' perception of the resulting fabric; buildings as urban markers of history and culture, and as creators of unique places within the city.

OPPOSITE Looking toward site along 125th Street at the height of Harlem Renaissance

ABOVE Rendered zoning envelope overlaid on rendered program provided by Jonathan Rose Companies

A major studio objective was to model the developer-architect relationship, including how we actually meet and present and exchange ideas. Jonathan Rose is the rare client that every architect competes to work with. This was an opportunity to see what it's like to interact, be pushed, and deepen one's work in response to such a client.

Architects are often in a position of inwardness/outwardness, where they attempt to understand the project both from the perspective of the developer and occupants and from the viewpoint of the larger context.

A constant objective of this studio was to explore the added value that a disciplined designer can bring to the developer's financial and building needs as well as to the project's larger societal mission. The final result was to be an articulated architectural construct anchored in this specific place and mission that accepted the development-process constraints while satisfying the highest standards of architecture.

OPPOSITE Seventh Avenue, looking north from West 125th Street, in Harlem, New York City, 1934. Schomburg Center for Research in Black Culture, Photographs and Prints Division, The New York Public Library. New York Public Library Digital Collections.

ABOVE Theatre, Music Hall, 125th St. near 8th Avenue, 1903. Byron Company (New York, N.Y.) / Museum of the City of New York. 41.420.378

OVERLEAF Apollo Theater, 253 West 125th Street, ca. 1978. Edmund Vincent Gillon / Museum of the City of New York. 2013.3.1.253

FLORSHEIM

APOLLO
APOLLO
SYLVERS BEG SEPT 20
ENCHANTMENT
SYLVERS
ENCHANTMENT
BEG SEPT 20
APOLLO
STEAK
LORDS

The Assignment

The Site

Jonathan Rose Companies was the development manager on behalf of the Upper Manhattan Empowerment Zone (UMEZ), which invested in the project to strengthen the presence of Harlem-based organizations that enrich the cultural life of the community and advance its economic development. The challenge was to help UMEZ conceptualize an extraordinary building that integrated a complex program on a tight site with iconic contextual solutions providing both economic and social returns on investment. The priority for the client stakeholders was to approach the project from the larger context of Harlem's dynamically evolving cultural identity in terms of its legendary past as the premiere African-American neighborhood in the United States; its prior history as a neighborhood of immigrants and its present as an explosively gentrifying district of Manhattan; 125th Street as a cultural center transitioning to a major retail street. One goal of the project was to balance the ratio of cultural and retail elements. Cultural tenants in the building included Firelight Media, a film producer that focuses on pivotal

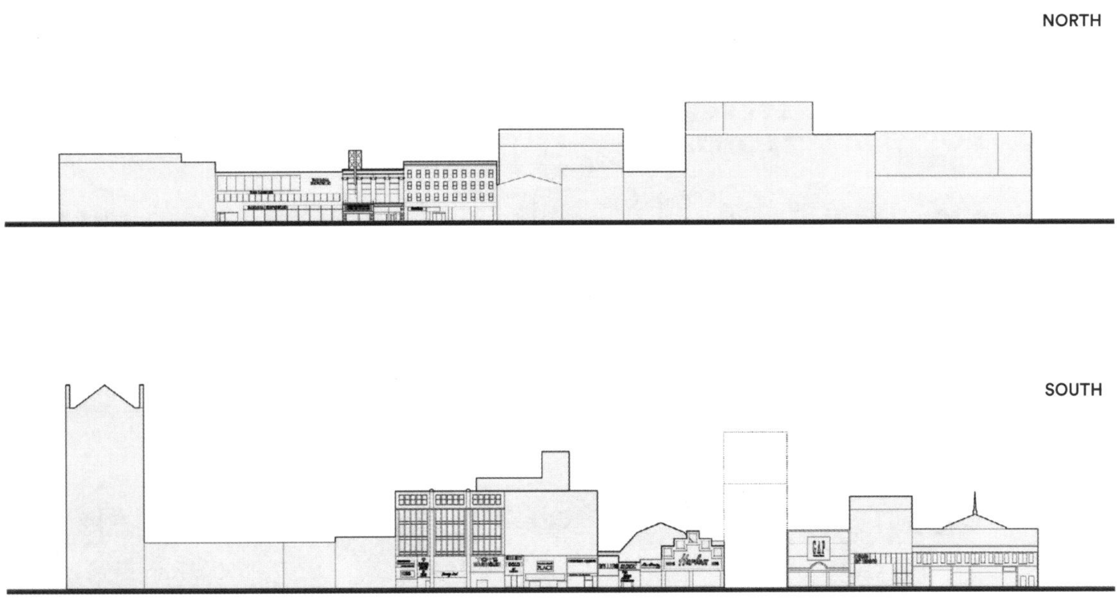

ABOVE 125th Street context elevations

moments of American history, and Futuro Media Group, an organization telling Latino stories overlooked by mainstream media.

The Program

The program was split between residential and cultural functions. The residential aspects required a disciplined use of structural geometry and planning for maximum efficiency of construction. The living units involved considerations of livability within relatively confined areas, maximization of fresh air and daylight, access to outdoor spaces, and special considerations with regard to acoustics that would allow its resident musicians to practice. Given the program mix, the cultural elements were complex to configure because they would compete for lobby space and 125th Street frontage.

Residential Program (124th Street) in 40,000 gross square feet

- 34 units of housing
- 124th Street residential lobby
- Communal arts space for resident use
- Laundry facility for resident use
- Other support spaces as required (storage, trash/recycling, etc.)

The programs were the result of zoning test-fit studies. For instance, the thirty-four housing units were a particular mix (eight studios, twenty-five one-bedrooms, and one two-bedroom) comprising one scenario of what could fit within the as-of-right floor-area ratio, height, and bulk requirements. These buildings are inefficient, so the net-to-gross ratio was going to be high.

Cultural/Commercial Program (125th Street) in 27,000 net square feet/35,000 gross square feet

125th Street lobby, approximately 1,000 net square feet
- Publicly accessible
- Visitors' kiosk managed by NYC & Co.
- Space to showcase works produced by building occupants

Screening room, about 2,000 net square feet
- Approximately 125 seats
- Multipurpose meeting room, approximately 1,000 net square feet
- Flexibility to host a variety of meetings and functions

Restaurant, approximately 7,500 net square feet
- On the 125th Street frontage
- Serves both building occupants and the general public

Futuro tenant space, approximately 3,000 net square feet
- Office and creative workspace, including media production facilities, meeting and administrative spaces

Required Square Feet for Each Program

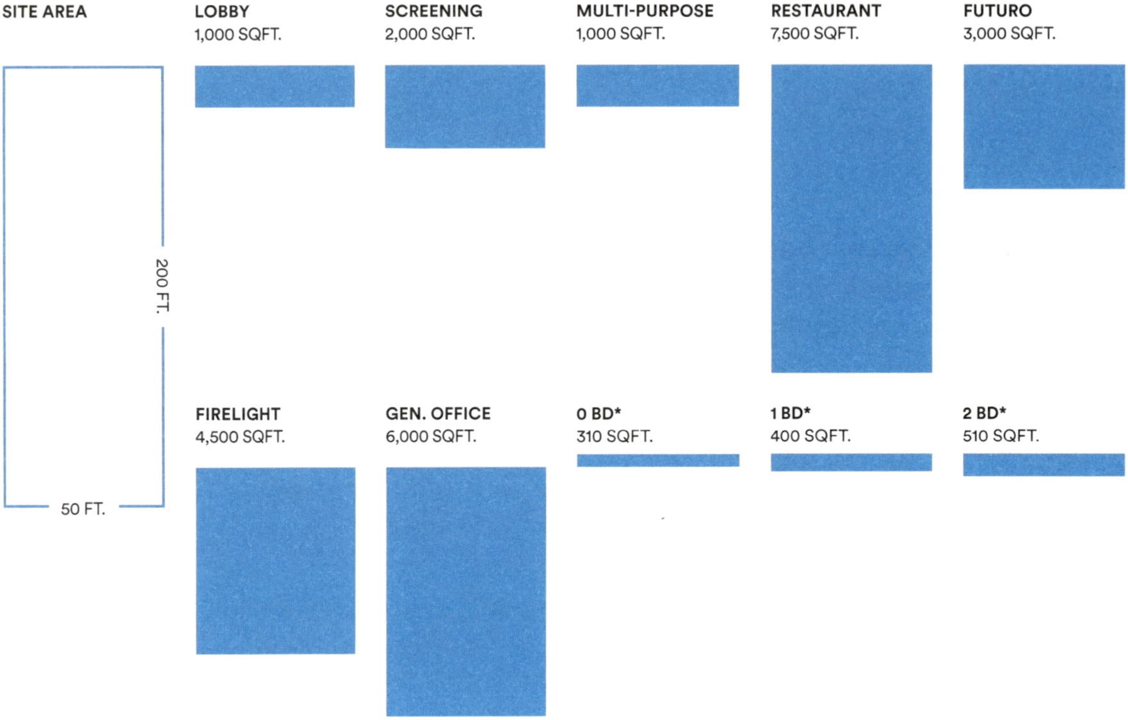

*BASED ON HPD MINIMUM NUMBERS FOR NEW CONSTRUCTION

Unit Mix Requirements for Residential Building

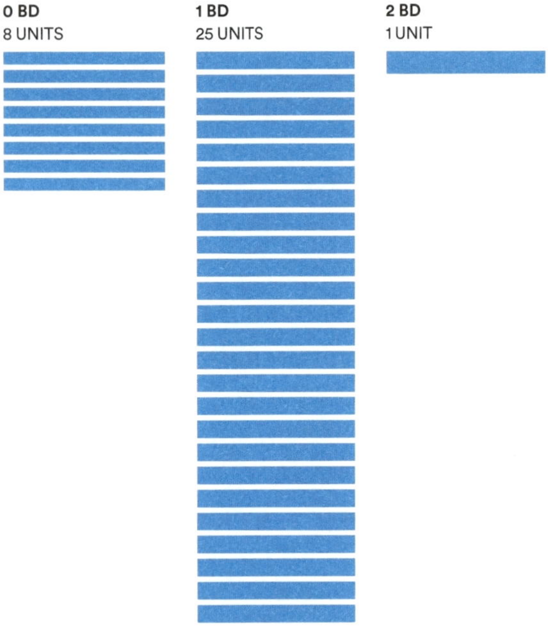

OPPOSITE, ABOVE Program diagram of cultural building

OPPOSITE, BOTTOM Program diagram of residential building

ABOVE Apollo Theater Africa Now! Concert 2016

- Serves Futuro staff, guests, and public

Firelight tenant space, approximately 4,500 net square feet
- Office and creative workspace, including media production facilities, meeting and administrative spaces
- Firelight staff, guests, and public

Spec office space, approximately 6,000 net square feet
- Office and creative workspace for media and arts organizations

Other support spaces (for storage and maintenance, etc.)

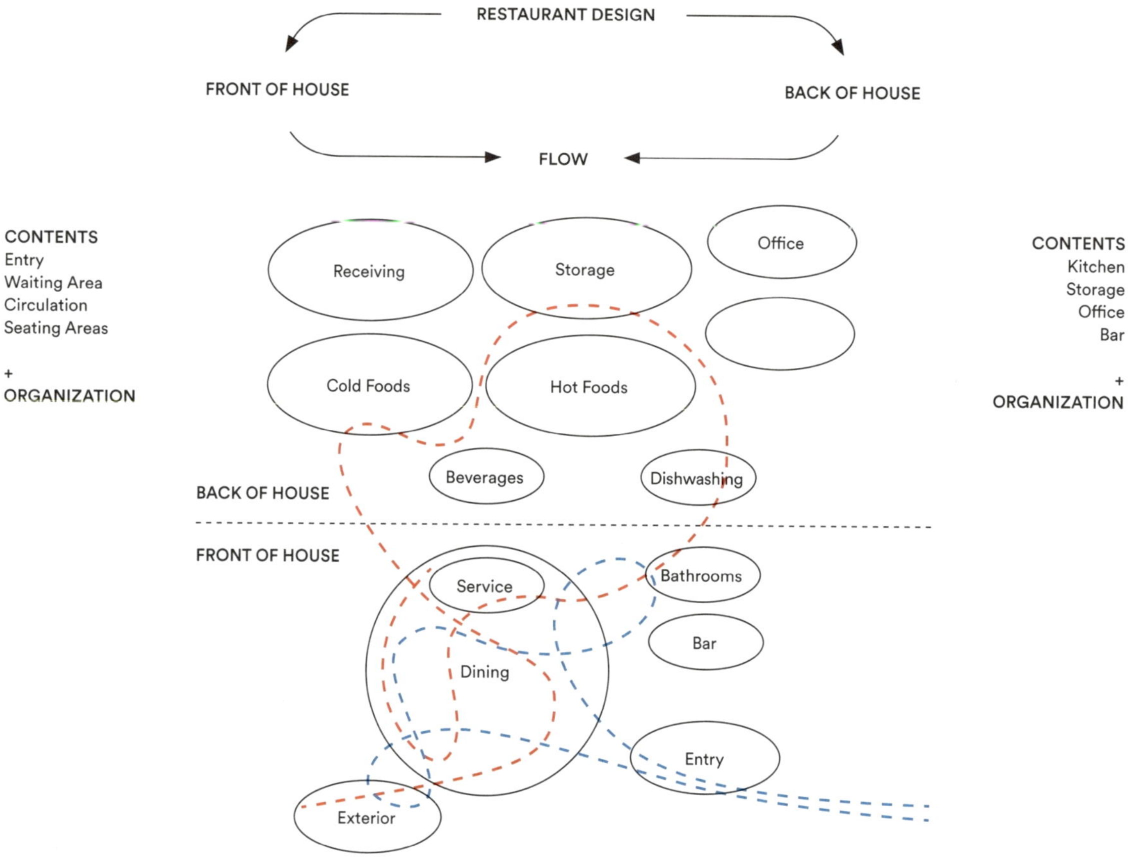

ABOVE **Restaurant spatial zoning and circulation flow research**

OPPOSITE **Daylight diagram superimposed on site**

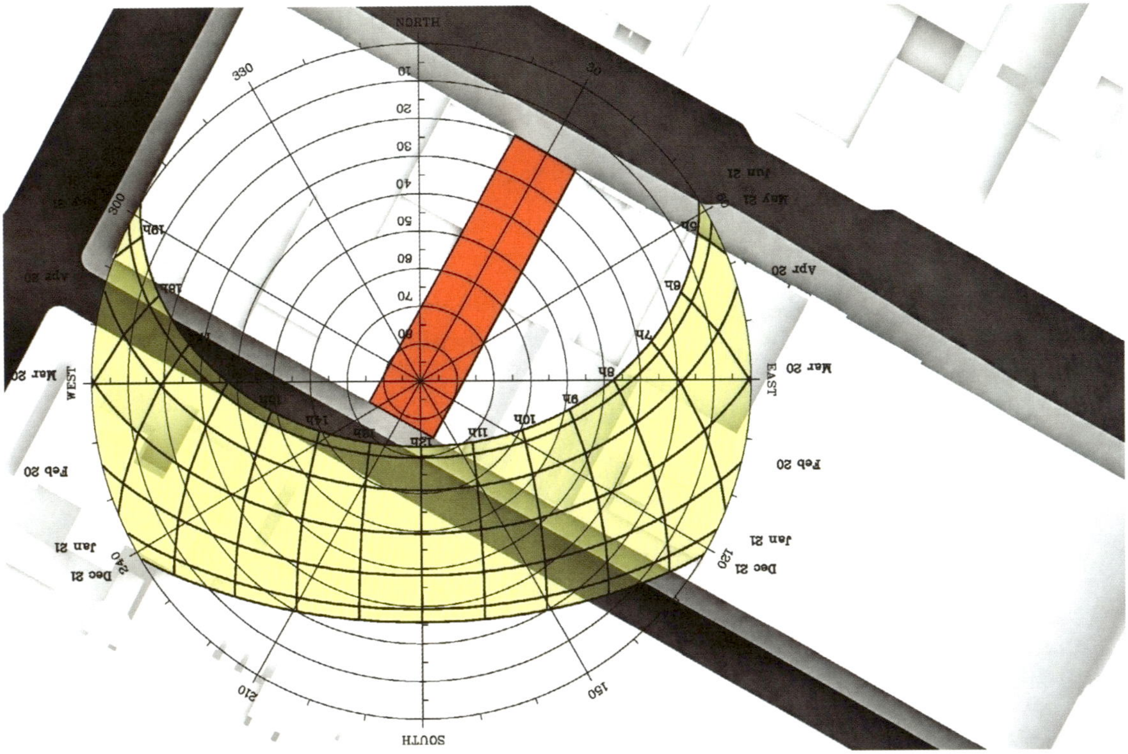

Work Plan

As an implementation-focused project, it required intensive and rapid development of schemes. During the first two weeks students worked in small teams to study the project's design constraints, including residential design, sustainable techniques of enclosure and construction, methods of delivering direct and indirect daylight, contemporary media production studio requirements, changing modalities of film and small performance presentation, and the cultural and physical history of the site and its surroundings. They also completed 3-D documentation of zoning constraints.

During the first week the students built a wood context model and, in teams of two, completed research on the following:

- residential design precedents at the apartment level, including indoor/outdoor spaces, taking into account HPD Design Guidelines for Multifamily New Construction and examples of roof and courtyard use;
- passive-house, sustainable techniques of enclosure and construction, and getting the facade right; methods of delivering direct and indirect daylight, natural ventilation, solar shading, solar energy for small buildings, and

REAR-YARD EQUIVALENT

"Any building or portion of a building used for any permitted use other than residences within a required yard. . . shall not exceed one story, excluding basement, nor in any event 23 feet above curb level. In addition, decks, parapet walls, roof thickness, skylights, vegetated roofs, and weirs, pursuant to Section 33-42 (Permitted Obstructions), shall be permitted above such a building."

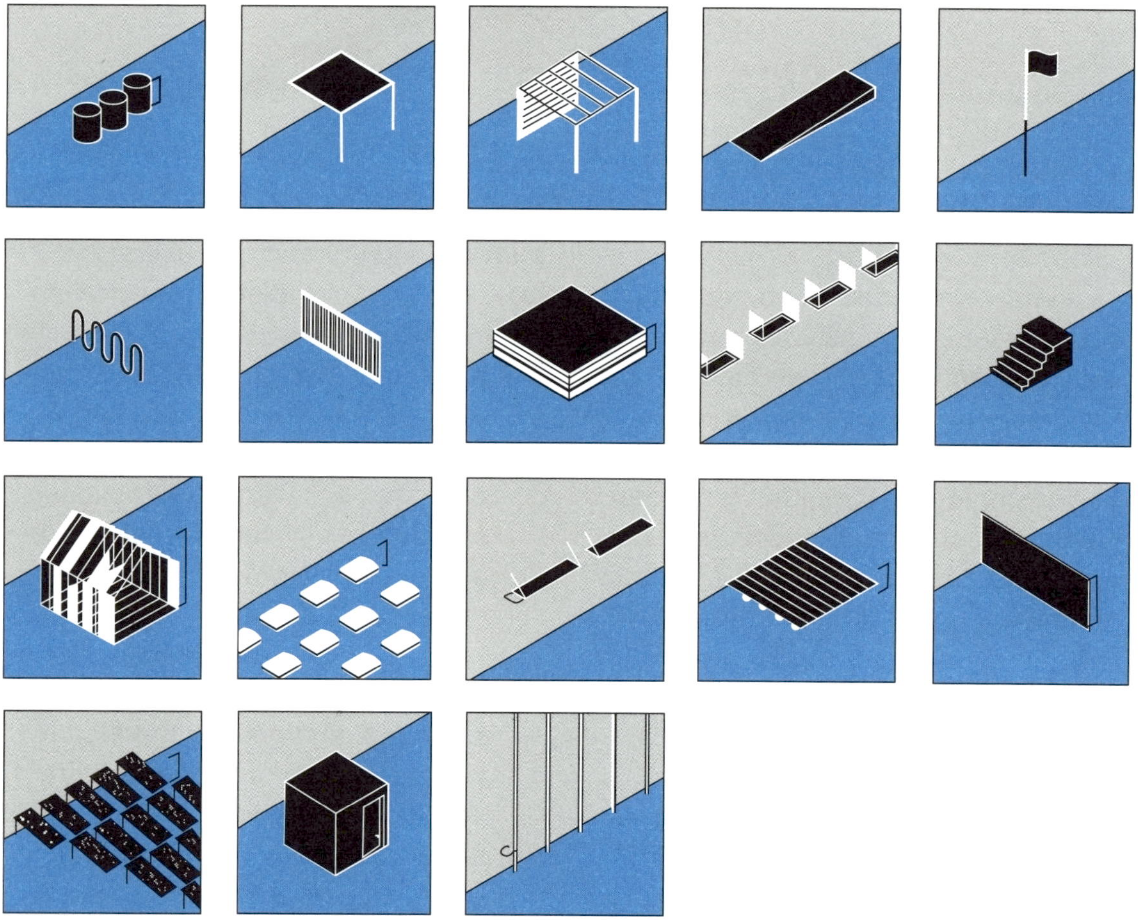

sustainable mechanical systems;

- restaurant design including components and flow of food service, what makes the front and back of the house function well, and farm-to-table in urban buildings;
- contemporary media production studio requirements and changing modalities of film and small performance presentation with interviews at Firelight and Futuro studios;
- cultural and physical history of the site and its surroundings, visual documentation of site and context including key historical Harlem and jazz landmarks, site demographics and urban context, 3-D site documentation of zoning constraints, reimagining Harlem's cultural flourishing in the twenty-first century.

The students also learned about the structural, MEP, and budget constraints as well as how to write a pro forma. During the second week they assessed their first pin-up of apartment layouts and research presentations with guest Sarah Ashcroft, of Jonathan Rose Companies.

OPPOSITE Diagram of zoning exceptions, part of a graphic handbook by students mapping out ways the zoning envelope can be manipulated

In the following two weeks the students completed early scheme development, presenting to the developer and various user groups how they considered input from public officials, zoning and budget stipulations from the developer's team, and requirements for structural, MEP, theatrical, and acoustical specializations. They also prepared a site plan, a volumetric and spatial zoning diagram, and a concept model.

During the fourth week the students visited the site and presented initial models to their professors as well as Angela Howard and Joseph Gabriel, of Jonathan Rose Companies, and Kenneth Knuckles and Verdery Roosevelt, of UMEZ, focusing on their relationship to the urban context. At this point the projects included volumetric drawings, sun/shadow and reflectance studies, and concept models. This first assessment of whether the design assumptions were valid or required rethinking was followed by a trip to Paris and Marseilles to visit buildings that dealt with similar challenges within different cultural contexts.

After their return to Yale, the students devoted the following month to detailed elaboration of the schemes, culminating in the midterm review. Weekly desk crits focused on the project's reconsidered concept, refined massing, cultural spaces presented in a site plan, drawings of the cultural base, a typical residential floor plan, a north-south section, a massing diagram, and a new model.

Next the students focused on daylight penetration, a community theater within the building, corridors and stairwells, a model of one- and two-bedroom residential units, and perspectives from 125th and 124th Streets. At midterm they presented a detailed concept including a site plan, a typical residential floor plan, a massing diagram, residential-unit and facade drawings, perspectives from 125th and 124th Streets, an aerial perspective, a one-unit interior perspective, and a model with development of all facades to a jury comprised of Emily Abruzzo, Tim Altenhof, Sara Caples, Alex Garvin, Andrei Harwell, Everardo Jefferson, Tessa Kelly, Kenneth Knuckles, Robert Marino, Jonathan Rose, and Elihu Rubin.

The project's second rigorous test informed the ensuing three weeks of final reworking and development of the schemes, while the last two weeks following fall recess were concentrated on robust graphic and 3-D communication of the designs. The resulting artifact, presented with detailed renderings and models, was to be a highly specific work of architecture. The students continued with pin-ups of detailed concepts and new models. For a group presentation of the building-as-cultural-anchor they now called "The Mark," they showed a larger-scale exploration of at least one major elevation with respect to materials and sustainability, and a drawing and model of one major space. They also attended lectures on estimating by Angela Howard, of Jonathan Rose Companies, on ornament by Yale professor Kent Bloomer, and on contemporary African-American artists by Sara Caples. Studio work was interspersed with visits to New York to see Rose Associates' Via Verde and meet restaurateurs Derek Fleming, of Red Rooster, and Danny Meyer, of Union Square Hospitality Group.

The final review was presided over by Sara Caples, Vincent Chang, Lisa Gray, Angela Howard, Julie Iovine, Everardo Jefferson, Kenneth Knuckles, Steven Lewis, Alan Organschi, Terence Riley, Verdery Roosevelt, Jonathan Rose, and Madlen Simon. Each student presentation included a site plan, cultural floors, typical residential floors, a cross section (both in perspective format and in context), elevations of 125th and 124th Streets, a massing diagram, a circulation diagram at the urban level, perspectives from 125th and 124th Streets, a perspective of a major space, a one-unit perspective, study and large-scale models, and a final model to be dropped into a context model. At least one of the drawings had to address the issues of The Mart.

EGRESS ELEMENTS
1. Exit and Exit Access
2. Exit Clearances and Obstructions
3. Stair Heights, Landings, and Roof Access
4. Stair Treads
5. Exit Discharge

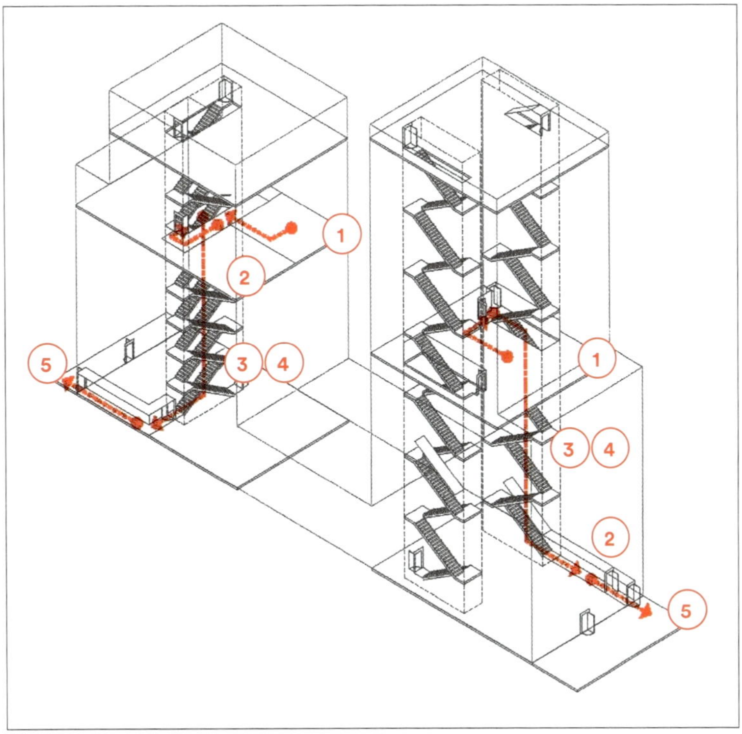

ABOVE Diagram of egress elements, part of an illustrated handbook by students mapping out code circulation requirements for safety and handicapped accessibility

OVERLEAF Cross section of uses presented to UMEZ

Student Work

Eunil Cho/ Jessica Elliott/ Dov Feinmesser/ Kirk Henderson/ James Kehl/ Jenny Kim/ Jeannette Penniman/ Melody Song/ Katherine Stege/ Xinyi Wang

Eunil Cho
Heart of Harlem

The Heart of Harlem project aims to strengthen the presence of Harlem-based organizations that both enrich the cultural life of the community and advance its economic development. Situated across the street from the Apollo Theater, the building inevitably engages with it both programmatically and visually. The entry sequence of the building acts as an extension to the Apollo Theater with its central axis aligned to the iconic marquee. Off this central circulation spine is a series of gathering spaces and performance stages that transition from public to private functions. The nucleus is a gracious restaurant and lounge that pays homage to the famed venues from the Harlem Renaissance with a circular central stage that can be easily transformed into a large performance space. A sunken courtyard brings daylight into the main restaurant space while offering privacy from adjacent buildings and visual relief from the busy 125th Street thoroughfare.

The complexity of the program required an architectural language both iconic and contextual to integrate the cultural center and senior housing units for retired jazz musicians on a tight site. The two buildings are mirrored in plan, section, and elevation to achieve continuity throughout the site and render the project as a singular structure. The facades of both buildings respond respectively to the program and natures of the two radically different streets while maintaining the same datum lines. The complex site program finds cohesion through a series of unique cultural community spaces and a clear architectural language that emulates both the past and the future of Harlem.

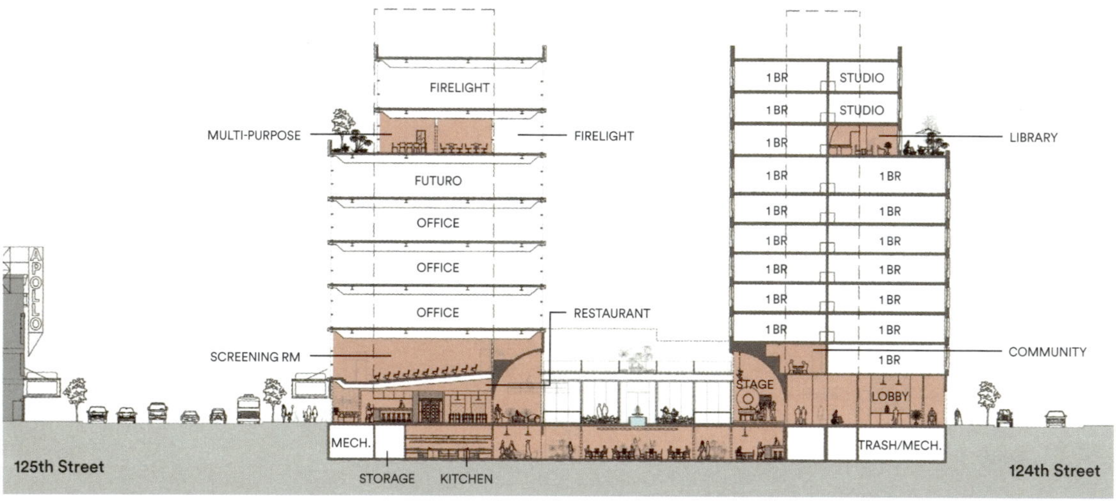

TOP Elevations on 125th Street, courtyard, and 124th Street

BOTTOM Section looking east

Restaurant and sunken courtyard

TOP & BOTTOM Courtyard perspectives

OPPOSITE Plans of the urban layer

LOWER LEVEL

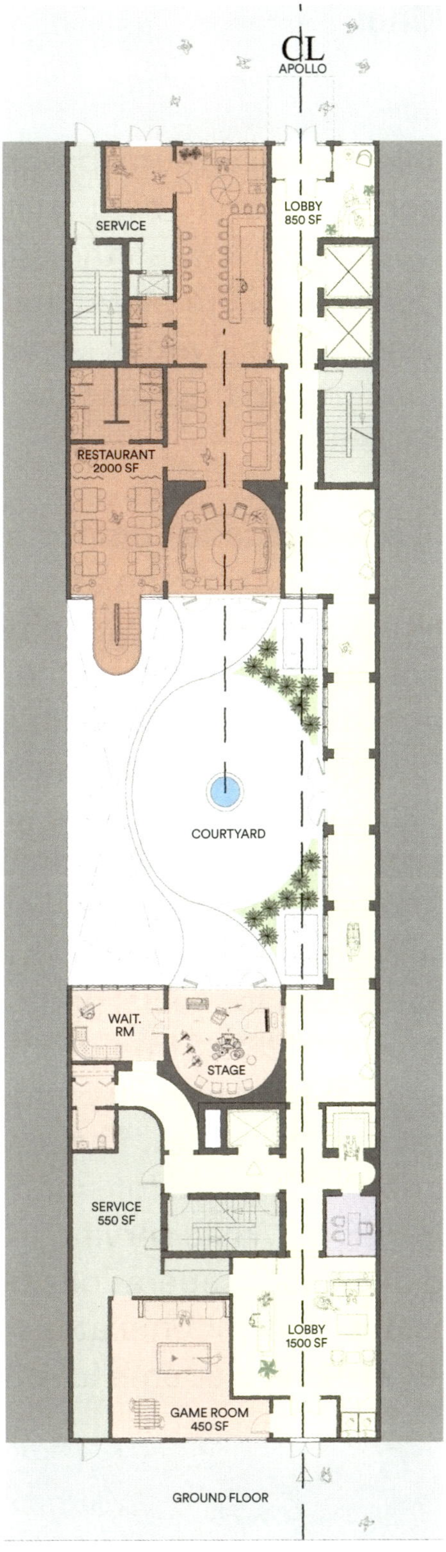

GROUND FLOOR

Jessica Elliot
Mark 125

With its injection of cultural programs, Mark 125 aims to represent and support the shifting cultural identity and potential of Harlem. The transparency between the double-height ground-floor restaurant and lobby on 125th Street and the cultural office spaces for Firelight and Futuro invites discovery from the street via a visual connection through the facade while promoting the creative economy of Harlem.

The 124th Street facade composition is reversed and scaled down at the entrance to serve the affordable-housing units and the intergenerational daycare amenity. To articulate the residential program of the second tower, the south elevation incorporates sun-shading devices allowing for light and heat-gain control. The courtyard, dedicated to the residents, includes a community garden with an undulating dichroic glass roof that can be observed from the restaurant below. Additional amenities, such as a gym and a community kitchen that look out onto the courtyard, promote health and wellness among residents while providing ample communal spaces for social gatherings. The restaurant occupies most of the 125th Street frontage, and a bar is located in the entrance to enhance visibility and draw patrons from the Apollo Theater, across the street. The main seating area of the restaurant functions as a stage for small performances underneath the dichroic skylight. While serving to mediate the desired connections and necessary separations between the private and public programs, the skylight emulates the beauty of diversity and unpredictability, evoking Harlem's identity and culture past and present.

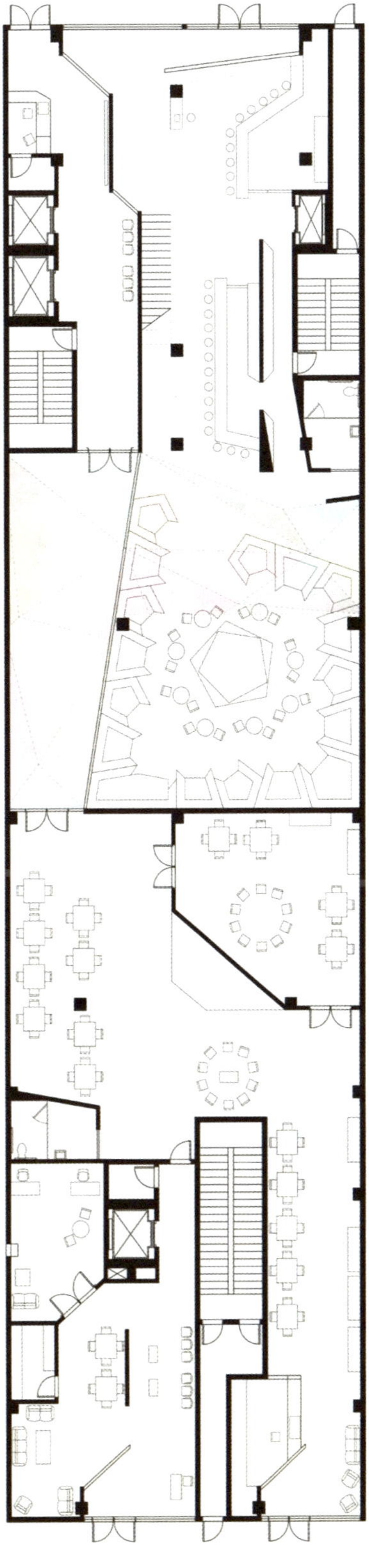

PREVIOUS PAGE Plans through the first and second levels.

OPPOSITE Restaurant model study

ABOVE Residential tower plans

OVERLEAF Section looking east

APOLLO
APOLLO THEATER
FIRELIGHT

Dov Feinmesser
Two Polarized Conditions

The Harlem Mart 125 project posed many challenges: the restrictive limitations of a financially viable development project, the professional and regulatory implications of constructing a mid-rise building in Harlem and the city of New York, the multilayered programmatic mix, and a position across from a landmark of American history, to name a few.

The proposed design addresses these parameters through a series of carefully choreographed spatial relationships unified by a single cohesive language. The residential building is comprised of an active ground level, including a large lobby that uses the sidewalk to create continuity between the building and the street, with a small commercial space that could serve as both income generator and amenity for residents. Behind the lobby is a large gathering area with a music room that can be opened up to extend into the courtyard and act as the focal point to the main public space.

Above are studios and one- and two-bedroom apartments, with layouts that allow for cross ventilation through the building, that could be easily transformed into larger units in the future. Midway up the building and at its top are amenity spaces that utilize the roof and setback terrace to provide views and spaces open to all residents. The residential tower is clad in a light brick that serves to blend it into the surrounding urban fabric and reflects the residential tone of the adjacent facades. The units facing the street all include customizable louver systems that allow residents to personalize their relationship to the outside.

The facade of the cultural component is an abstraction of work by local artists, forming a colorful yet subdued exterior that offers tenants privacy while respecting the iconic status of the Apollo Theater, across the street. The tower is topped by a bar offering expansive views to the north and south over Manhattan. The unifying goal of the buildings is to foster the sense of community embodied by Harlem's past.

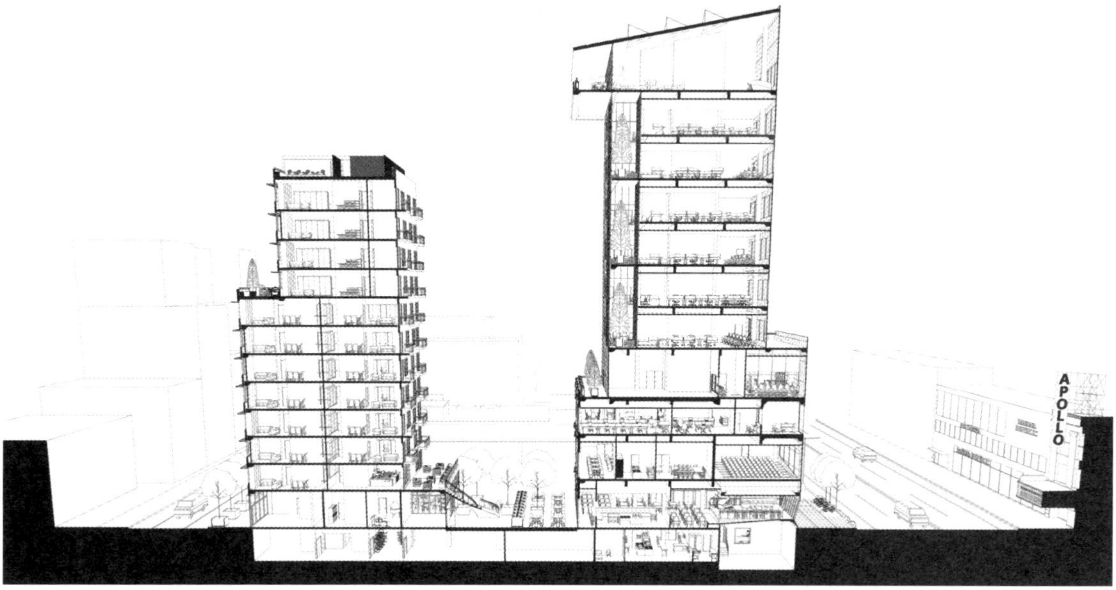

ABOVE Section looking west

OVERLEAF Elevations

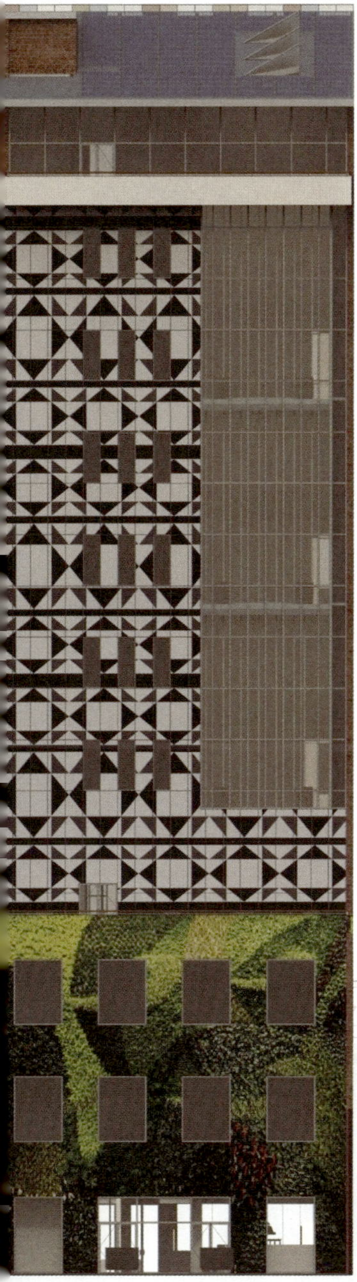

ABOVE Restaurant views

OPPOSITE View along 125th Street

GAP
Factory Store

Alex Garvin, Public Realm Strategist, in conversation with writer Colette Taber

Alex Garvin The goal of the Bass Studio is to teach students how the market works. As is the case with many developers participating in the studio program, Jonathan Rose was able to provide a solid overview of the market's mechanics. Rose knows how to manage restaurants and residential properties, and he knows how to move people and goods. Maximizing revenue is the central role of the developer, but what additional knowledge did students gain from working with Rose? The developer's background in urban planning makes all the difference; he received a master's degree in regional planning from the University of Pennsylvania in 1980. So they had access to a unique set of skills embodied in a trained planner. For example, Rose is capable of impressing on the students the importance of enhancing activity at the street level. The Harlem project's diverse program, which included commercial, residential, and cultural components, necessitated a command of circulation to engage people successfully both within and outside the proposed building.

Colette Taber I surmise that you are addressing a bigger idea when you suggest that architects in training could benefit from a planner's tutelage. Rose's career and writings suggest a

ABOVE Courtyard study model for first UMEZ presentation by Jessica Elliott

OPPOSITE 125th Street Elevation at midterm review by Xinyi Wang

lifetime commitment to ensuring that our cities, towns, and communities remain strong, vibrant places to live, work, and play. Serving as the studio's developer, he represented a rare opportunity to learn about the "reality of the private market" in a socially and environmentally conscious context.

AG The students' grasp of the Harlem neighborhood—and specifically the portion of West 125th Street where the Apollo Theater resides—was expectedly lacking. Their knowledge of the historical and cultural context was naive at best.

CT What about the development's frontage on 125th Street?

AG This aspect of the studio project, centered on the residential component, was ripe with potential for referencing

history in a high-density, pedestrian-friendly environment in interesting and innovative ways. Similarly the juxtaposition of commercial and residential programs on busy 124th Street provided an opportunity to capitalize on heavy pedestrian traffic.

CT How did the students' schemes miss the historical and/or cultural mark?

AG I remember them as more design oriented; the history felt incidental. The students' 3-D solutions were very sophisticated. The problem lies in the fact that many of the designs could work equally well on another street, in another neighborhood, in another city.

CT Your unusual insight into Harlem's special attributes is the result of a personal relationship with the neighborhood. How did you learn so much about it, aside from playing a role in the neighborhood's redevelopment as a professional city planner?

AG I studied the area while working on my architecture degree in city planning at Yale. I have read Harlem's literature and walked its streets. And I have cherished childhood memories rooted in the neighborhood's history: Sugar Ray Robinson's pink Cadillac parked outside his bar, on Seventh Avenue and 124th Street, and glimpses of Fidel Castro at Hotel Theresa in 1960. It is very difficult to separate these images from the site.

In terms of Yale's educational traditions, I liked the definition Sara Caples put forth: "The idea is not to train people to have a single approach to architecture, but to teach them how to think as architects." I diverge from her explanation in one way perhaps, in terms of the encouragement of "developing different techniques." Different "thinking" can be an inherent by-product of this pursuit. There is a schism between the academic classroom and the studio, where the developer's input addresses missing practical components such as how to get a building

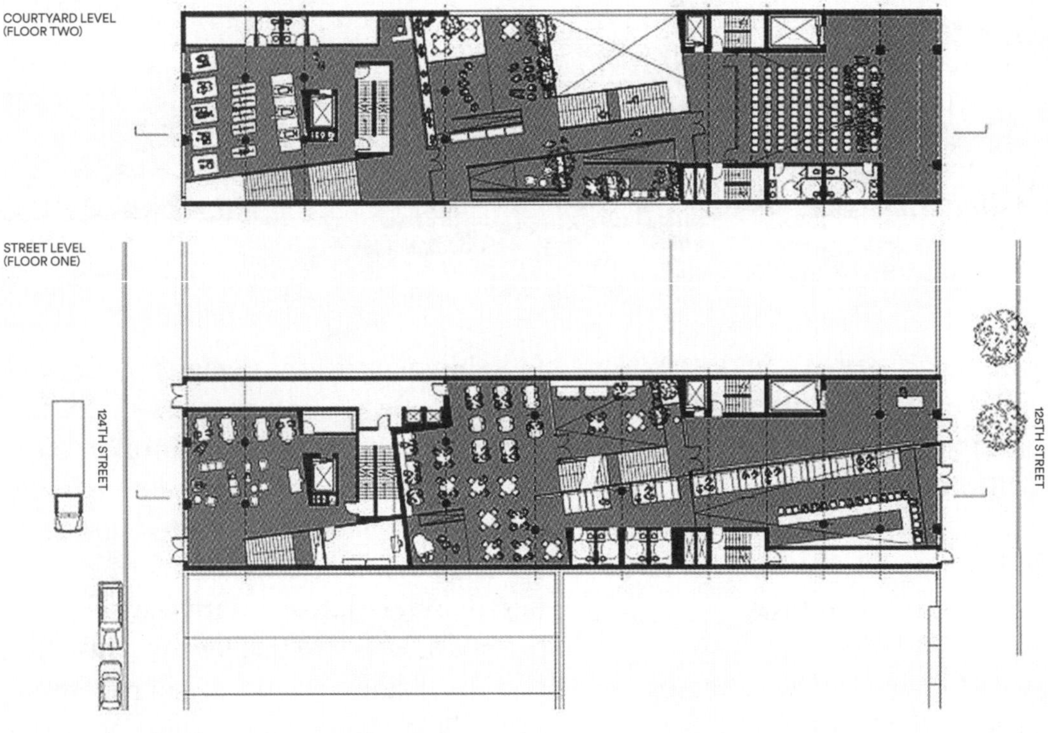

ABOVE Restaurant plan, UMEZ study, by Jeannette Penniman

OPPOSITE Alex Garvin at midterm review of Katherine Stege

built and, just as important, how to manage a property after completion. It is of critical importance for architects to understand how to finance construction, which typically requires strategies for the approvals process.

The employment of varied techniques for community engagement also requires merging the public and private realms. A diverse program such as that put forth for the Harlem project can be a catalyst for maximizing revenue through leveraging the activity (and energy) of adjacent public spaces. The proposed restaurant has a high level of activity to be harnessed. I counsel clients to ask themselves, "How do you enhance activity?" One of the most effective techniques is to allow passersby to see into a building through the use of transparent materials at the street level. Similarly alcoves, rain canopies, and U-shaped windows help break down the division between public and private spaces. Architects need to think about "all the spaces that we occupy and share" when designing.

Kirk Henderson
Harlem Eye

The UMEZ redevelopment plunges a new civic-oriented building into the turbulent spatial and social waters of Harlem's 125th Street. Sitting midblock across from the Apollo Theater, the building promises to stand not as a beacon of resistance to change but as a living totem for a future borne of gathering, conversation, creation, and communal dwelling.

At a time when Harlem's traditional community bonds are weakening and the social and commercial demand for physical event spaces is at an all-time high, Mart 125 must above all serve as a conduit for the types of human assembly that facilitate an equitable and convivial, if unknown, future. This project seeks to blueprint the spatial and architectural groundwork for the built infrastructure of that future. To this end it is a study in the careful programming of intimate gathering, from the private to the communal.

A portico is recessed off the sidewalk to welcome passersby to an information booth, a takeaway beverage stand, and relief from the chaos of 125th Street. From there French-style double-glass doors open to offer the visitor a range of options. The café bar extends through the middle of the building; peripheral hallways lead to the office elevators and event space at the rear; a grand staircase rises to the formal restaurant on the second floor, which connects to the street via two platforms on a mezzanine-level balcony overlooking the café. The left passage brings visitors past the food retail outlets to a vast two-story event space with an encircling balcony and large circular skylight. The skylight suffuses the space with daylight from the garden terrace above, visually linking to the two halves of the site. Each space is characterized by aspects of the familiar and the new, and the functional yet transformative, as a way to sustain enduring interactions between people throughout the project's lifetime.

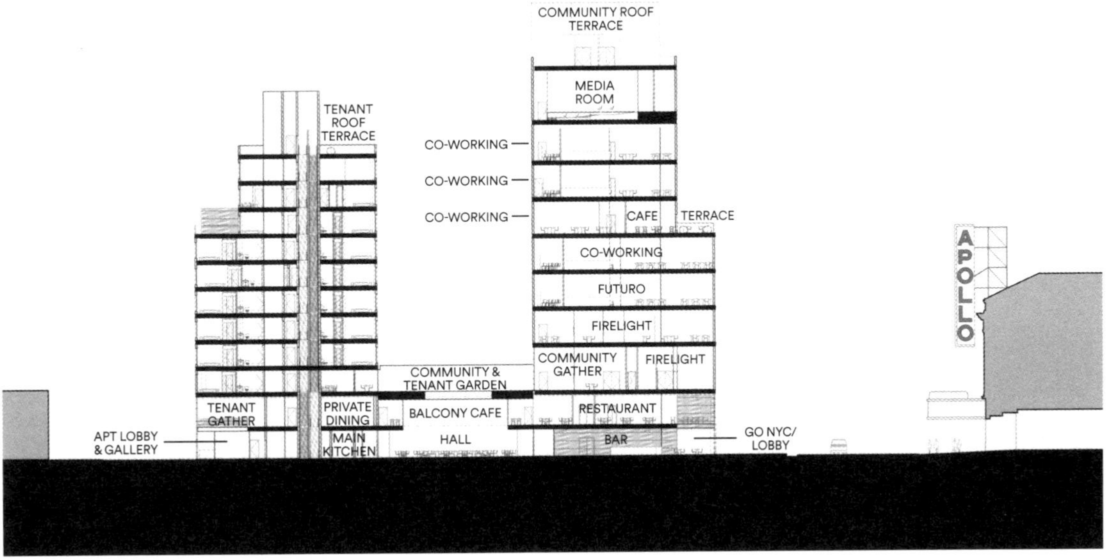

Section looking west

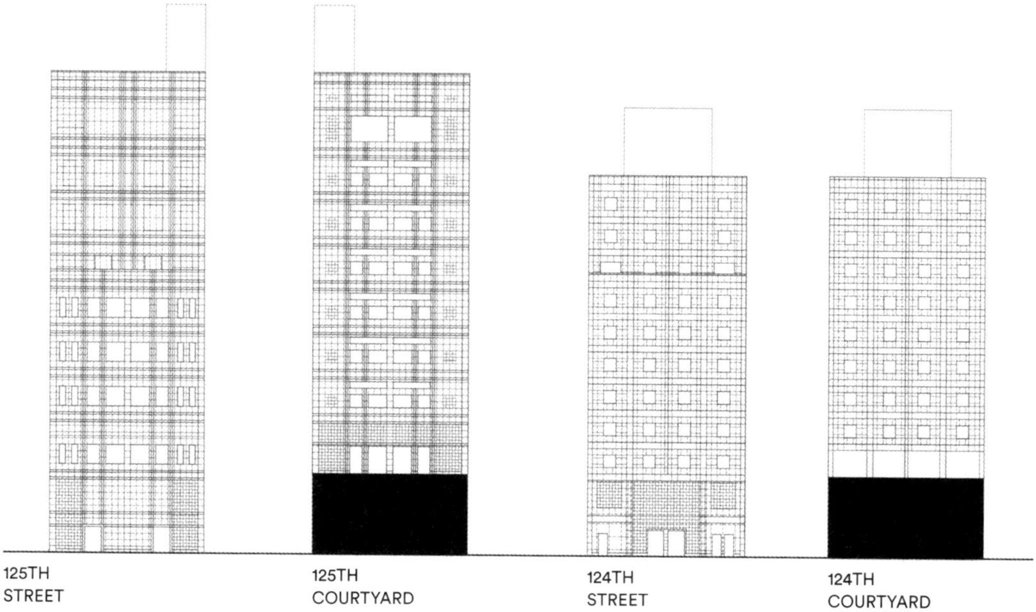
125TH
STREET
125TH
COURTYARD
124TH
STREET
124TH
COURTYARD

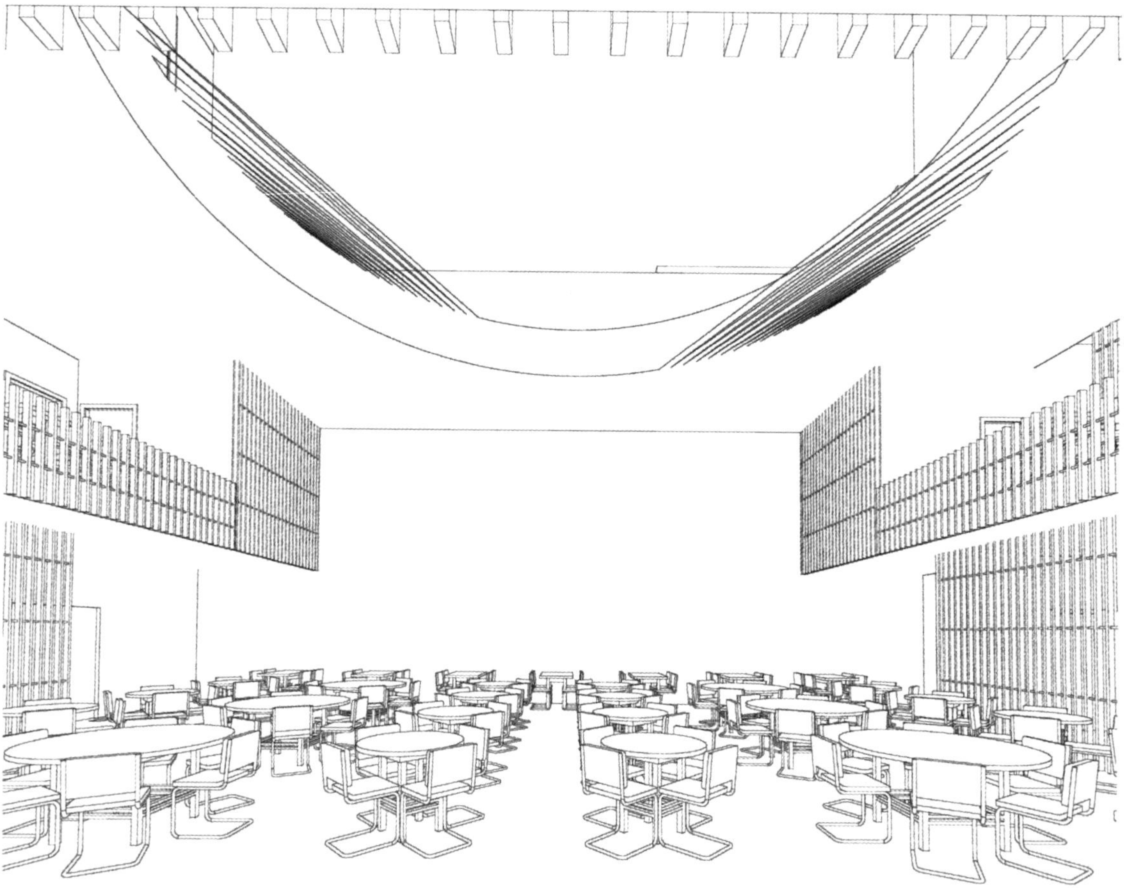

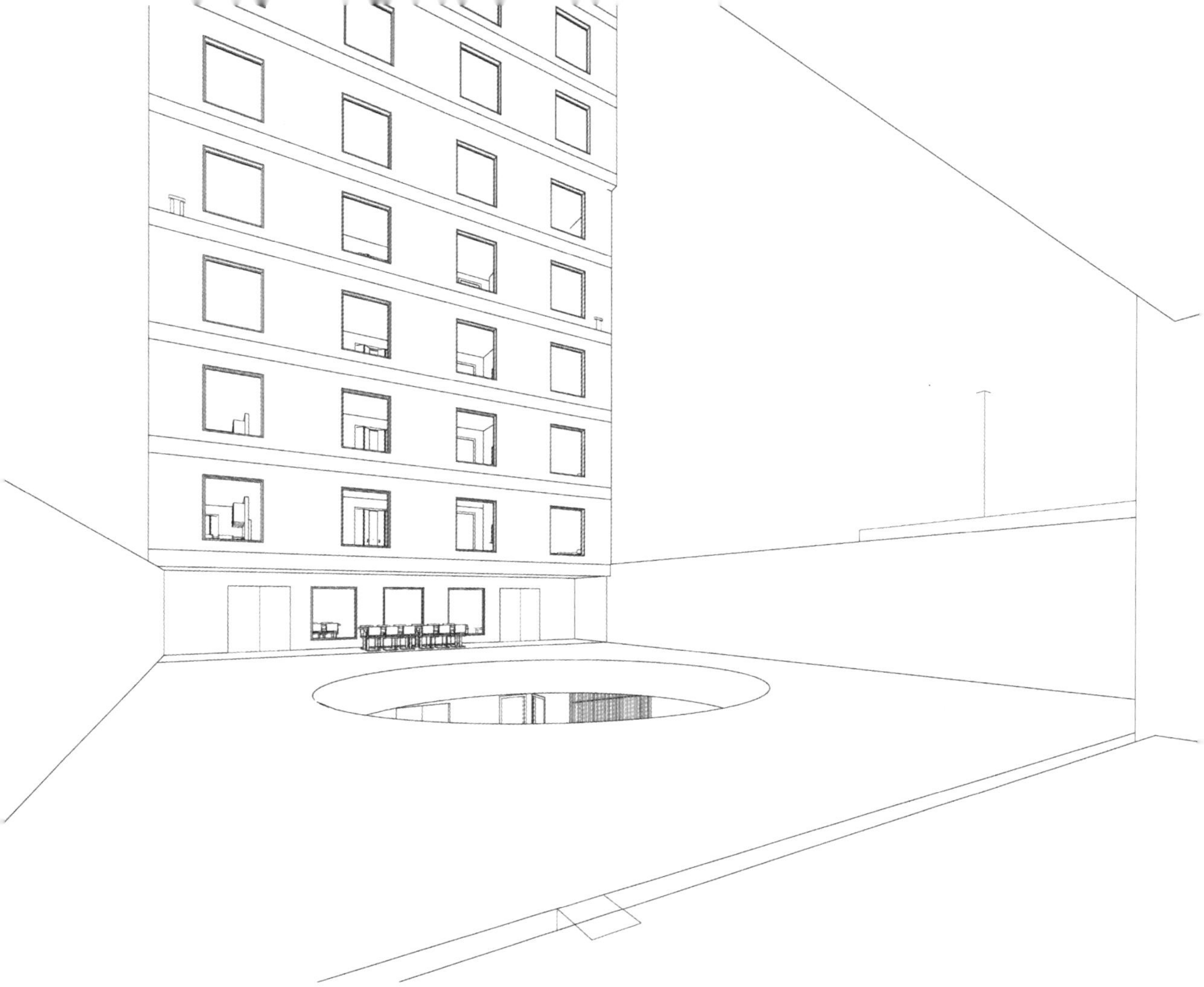

OPPOSITE TOP Elevations

OPPOSITE BOTTOM Restaurant perspective of the Eye

ABOVE Community courtyard perspective of the Eye

James Kehl
Urban Layers

The site is situated on a narrow through lot that connects two polarized conditions: the commercial activity of 125th Street and residential facilities on 124th Street with scant building frontage and community presence. This project design negotiates and engages with the diverse characters of the two streets through conceptual urban layers at the building's vertical street walls and continuous ground level.

On 125th Street, the building's commercial and cultural side, a space created by a fifteen-foot-deep street wall (generated through a required setback) hosts collaborative office areas made divisible by curtains that could be used for digital projection screens. Media content generated by artists or building tenants could be cast onto these curtains, illuminating the north facade at night to enhance the vibrant street life. This vertical layer resolves itself at the ground level as a series of frames: the box-office, the office and restaurant entryways, and a performance stage, which contributes to the dynamic cultural character of the street. In contrast, the 124th Street side becomes a vertical garden that enlivens an otherwise dead urban space. A layer of sunrooms covered with plantings and a ground-level oasis and porch create a focal point for engagement between the building's tenants and the community.

The vertical layers are connected through a specially programmed continuous ground level. On 125th Street there is a restaurant on the ground and basement levels, while on 124th Street there is a community space to serve residents. A courtyard in between the buildings (generated through a rear-yard requirement) mediates these actively programmed spaces. The ground level establishes strong continuity by aligning all utility, core, and service spaces against the southeast edge of the building, allowing for a clear visual passage through the restaurant and courtyard into the neighborhood beyond. Although the brief for this project demanded many diverse programs, a common thread is established via the definition of common architectural strategies and the creation of connective spaces.

Changeable elevation on 125th Street

Cultural and residential elevations on 124th Street

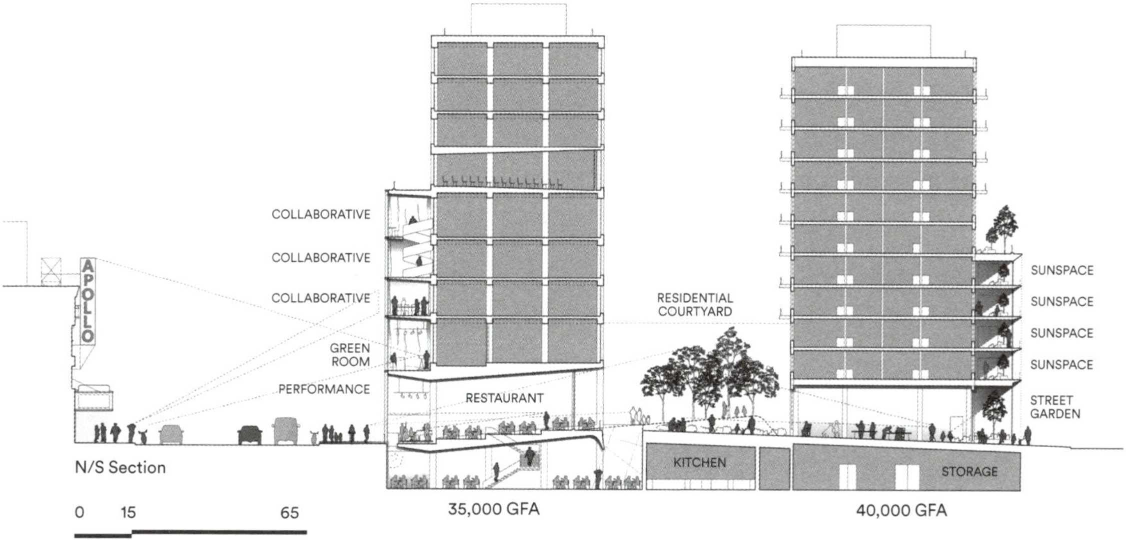

TOP Section looking east

BOTTOM Section model of urban layer

OVERLEAF View toward the Apollo

APOLLO
APOLLO
WELCOME TO THE WORLD
APOLLO THEATER

Jenny Kim
Creative Coexistence: A Proposal for Multigenerational Housing for Artists

The vitality of the Harlem Renaissance is still evident in our culture today. Many of the art and activist movements that defined the period emerged from spaces created by artists, musicians, activists, and writers. The proposed design aims to create a place for tenants not only to live but also to engage in the vibrant social sphere they are familiar with while creating a space that emulates the fluid and shifting pace of life during the Harlem Renaissance.

This project also aims to preserve the value of landmarks such as the Apollo Theater and equally to embody a strong presence as a new landmark on this historic street. The ground floor is dedicated to a public program that serves the community at large. The required setback from both sides of the lot allows space for a 3,000-square-foot central courtyard. The cultural venue has a restaurant and public exhibition space for Firelight, one of the required tenants. Both buildings open up into the courtyard, designed to be a series of "stages" shifting in scale and blurring the boundaries between the two different building programs.

Unit Flexibility

The Harlem Renaissance is often associated with formal cultural venues such as the Cotton Club, Savoy Ballroom, and Apollo Theater; however these venues represent only the performance and staging of the arts. The proposed design challenges the standard distribution of unit types to allow the capability of accommodating housing types from single occupants to small and large families, or even groups of artists, while meeting the required number of units. Smaller studio units may be combined with one-bedroom units to create two- or three-bedroom layouts, allowing the plans to grow and adapt according to the needs of the housing market.

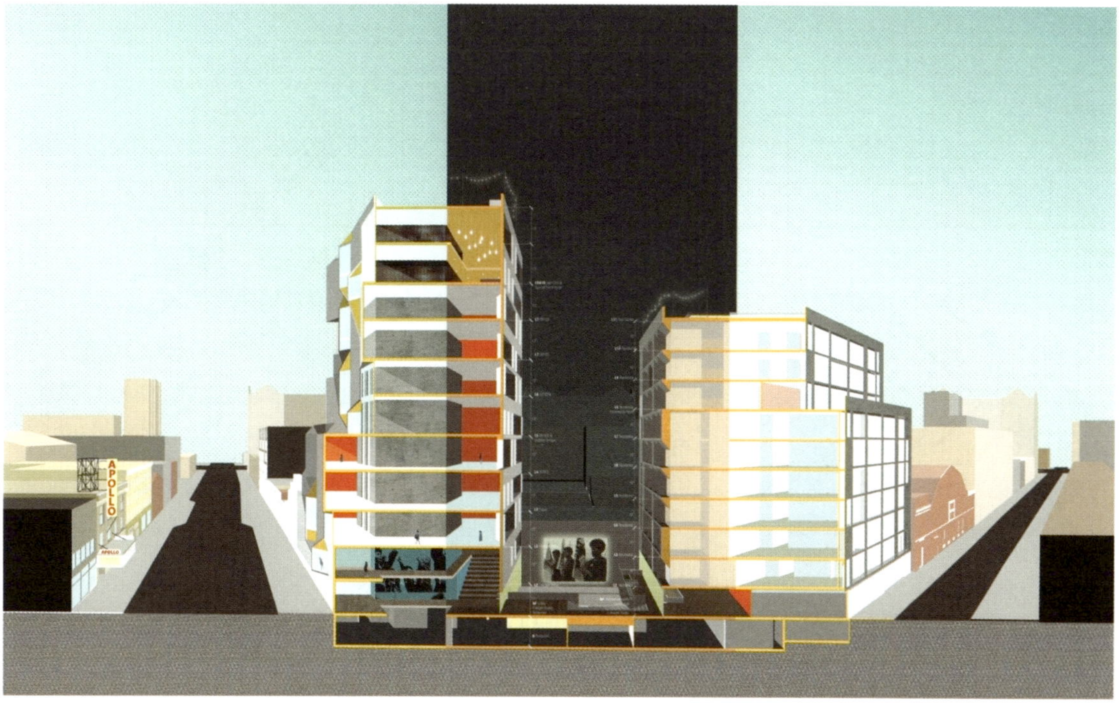

Section perspective looking east

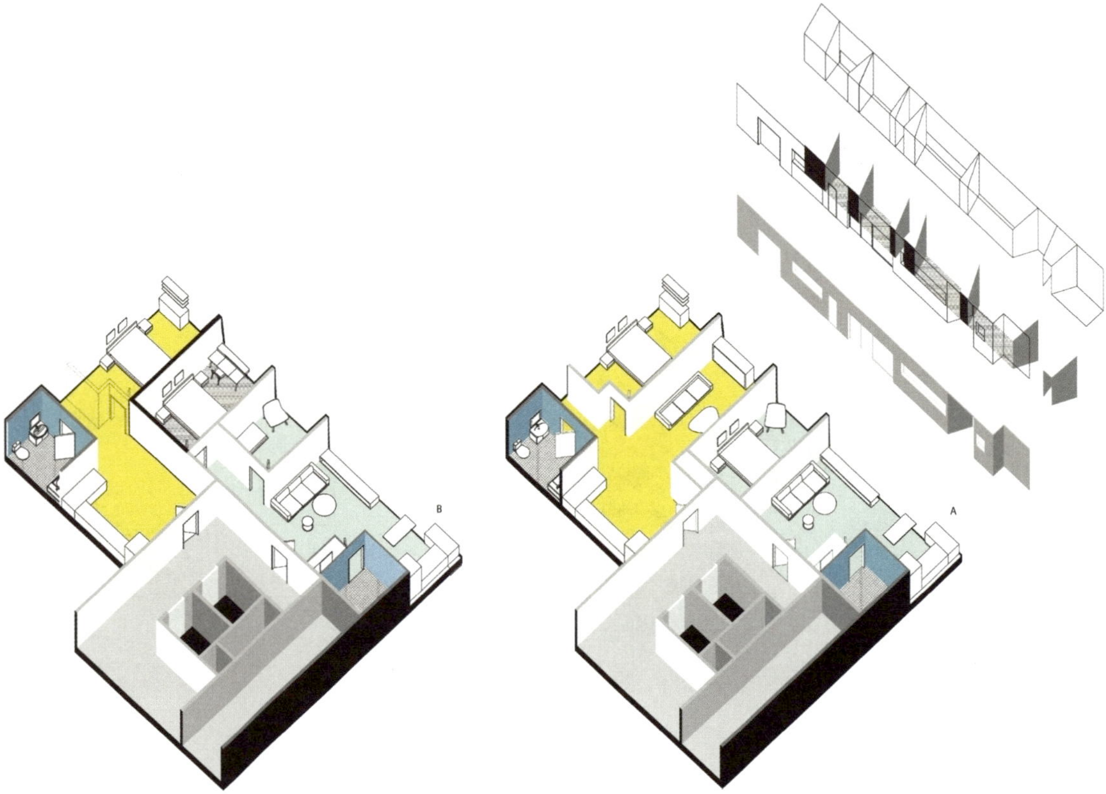

ABOVE Variable residential units

OPPOSITE Views into the courtyard as seen from a residential unit

ABOVE 125th Street facade study

OPPOSITE Model of courtyard and lobby

Reflections on the studio review by Steven Lewis, Urban Design Director, Planning and Development Department, City of Detroit

My reflections are narrowly focused based on the work the students presented at the final review. To a seasoned design professional, the constraints imposed by the client are viewed as opportunities to explore and exploit the facets of a project that can be expressed in various ways within the established boundaries. Sara and Everardo's students were challenged by the project's complex combination of programmatic, cultural, and economic criteria, a learning experience of great value as the conditions of practice are so often overlooked within the academy.

ABOVE UNIA parade, organized in Harlem, 1920

OPPOSITE Portrait of Thelonious Monk, Howard McGhee, Roy Eldridge, and Teddy Hill, Minton's Playhouse, New York, N.Y., ca. Sept. 1947. Photograph by William P. Gottlieb. Music Division, Library of Congress.

MINTON'S PLA

Harlem: **MART 125**

I was tickled by the foreign students who fell in love with African-American culture and attempted to reflect it in their designs following their research into Harlem's historical significance. However the depth of understanding required to honor that culture sufficiently is not attainable in such a short time. With so much to consider—Harlem's rich culture and history, Jonathan's program and budget, a tight site opposite one of the country's most iconic entertainment venues, and the students' paradigm of designing without limits—it is no wonder that the design responses were so varied, each with its own pluses and minuses. The tension created by layering the client's needs and objectives onto the basic design challenge forced the students to think outside of the normal sphere of expectations for a design studio.

OPPOSITE Mart 125, 2018

ABOVE Steve Lewis at final jury

Jeanette Penniman
Public Axis

The UMEZ redevelopment raised questions of gentrification and social sensitivity while presenting real opportunities for strengthening a rapidly evolving community. As sociologists have observed of Harlem and elsewhere, the perceived threat of gentrification is often a large part of its damage, and increasing the social enfranchisement of a neighborhood is only valuable if it can be shared across existing and newly arrived residents. Harlem—and notably its main artery 125th Street—is in many ways emblematic of the unease, resentment, and confused architecture that rapid gentrification produces.

It is in this changing social and architectural context that the proposal for a new Mart 125 positions itself as a physical link between new and existing communities. Half of the lot, fronting 125th Street, offers a series of office spaces for media nonprofits and other cultural tenants as well as a public screening room and large restaurant. The other half, facing 124th Street, offers thirty-four much needed affordable-housing units, in this case targeted for aging jazz musicians. Both sides of the site are designed around shared spaces meant to promote socialization and cross-pollination of ideas.

The material expression of the building seeks to respect the historical character of Harlem while distinguishing it as the neighborhood continues to change. Dark brick and an expressed structure balance the domestic nature of 124th Street with the institutional face of 125th Street. Although a tight zoning envelope limits the building's massing, exuberant metal profiles on both sides give the facade a sense of variation and character. These structures are functional and expressive, evoking some of the well-known artistic and architectural languages of Harlem (wrought iron and the smoke imagery of Aaron Douglas) and reflecting the activity within the building.

The heart of the building is the elevated central courtyard and public sequence running through the first two floors. Arranged along a strong diagonal, this sequence pulls commercial tenants, passersby, and the street's energy through a public lobby and light-filled sunken courtyard, which is shared with a lively bar and restaurant off of 125th Street. From 124th Street tenants can access the courtyard by moving up through a lobby and large fitness area. The courtyard offers a series of intimate spaces where people from all walks of life in Harlem can meet, both intentionally and accidentally. Mart 125 aims to capitalize on the striking demographic change evolving in central Harlem and increase a sense of agency and ownership among its neighbors.

Harlem: **MART 125**

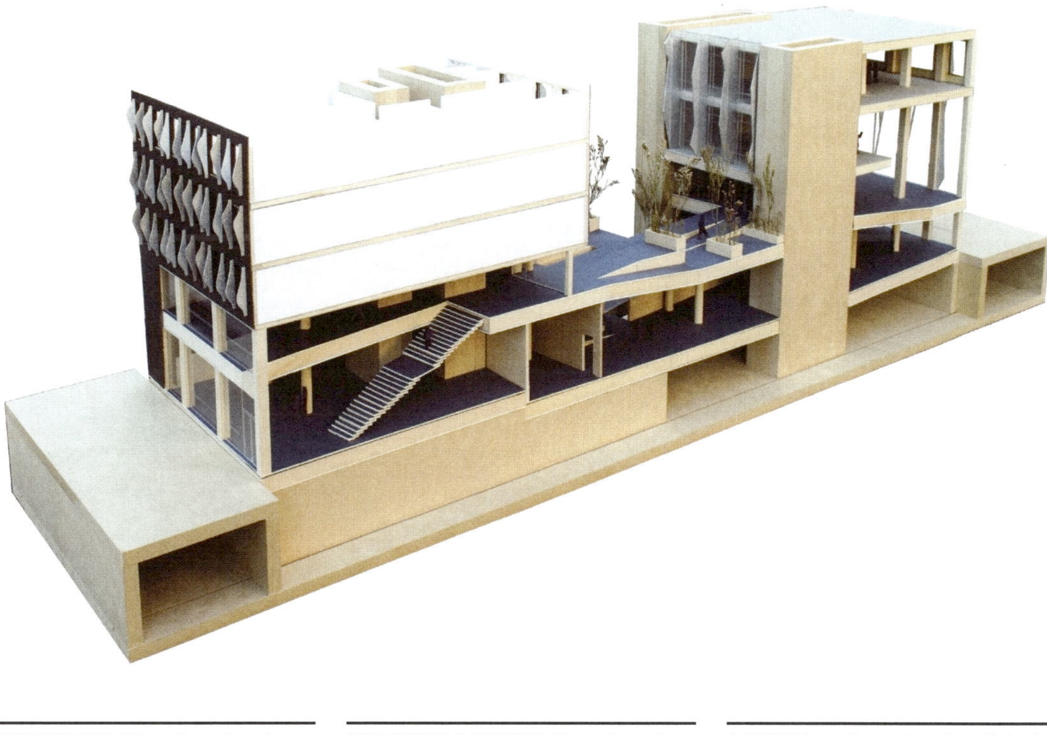

OPPOSITE TOP Elevation of residential building on 124th Street

OPPOSITE BOTTOM Elevation of cultural and commercial building on 125th Street

ABOVE Detail sectional model of base condition of building

Passage to the courtyard

Entering the courtyard

Melody Song
Home to Harlem

Maya Angelou once described Harlem as "the most dangerous crossroads of black America," just as it is the place where the Hotel Theresa rises tall and the legendary marquees of the Apollo and Victoria Theaters loom over the heads of passersby. As the hotbed of the Harlem Renaissance, its corners saw the first black American public theater, the rise of Malcolm X, the parades of the Black Elk, and the crowds cheering for Joe Louis. The era christened Harlem as home to the international African diaspora and, of even larger relevance, the embodiment of modern man's struggle with notions of liberty, identity, and citizenship. Although it is to be privately developed, the site is of public interest in terms of its need to herald the past as the grounds upon which the future is built. To accomplish this task the proposed building design includes a dramatic facade on 125th Street adorned by a vertical exhibit with a motif that recalls the Harlem Renaissance.

The fire escape, a ubiquitous feature of late-1800s brownstones and tenement buildings, is stylized into the form of a lightning bolt, a motif used by artist Aaron Douglas in religious paintings such as *The Judgment Day* (1939). The facade showcases Harlem's history and the work of media tenants Futuro and Firelight as a reflection of the street, recalling the performances and social interaction that took place at the star-studded Apollo.

The fire stair cuts into the interior courtyard as a connecting device that visually links the residential and office buildings. The housing complex is designed for maximum flexibility and co-living for senior jazz musicians. The bottom three floors are programmed as residency hotels to promote the mingling of visiting scholars and resident musicians. The residential building emulates, at a smaller scale, the qualities of Hotel Theresa that made it a cultural hothouse: a mixture of long-term and transient guests, minimized and collectivized household maintenance, and an engagement with the community beyond the nuclear family. Organized with a tight service core, the housing complex's spacious corridor living rooms are used for shared kitchen and lounge areas. Private units are designed with operable partitions to accommodate shrinking or growing families.

The proposed building complex also encourages the mingling of young and elderly residents, and shared programming among the media and housing complexes. It acknowledges text and media as critical elements of architecture, especially given the project of remembrance. Ultimately the architectural project at stake is an urban one. It celebrates the most original human impulse in a city, one that resonates with Harlem's history: to make a place and "name for ourselves, lest we be dispersed over the face of the whole earth" (Genesis 11:4).

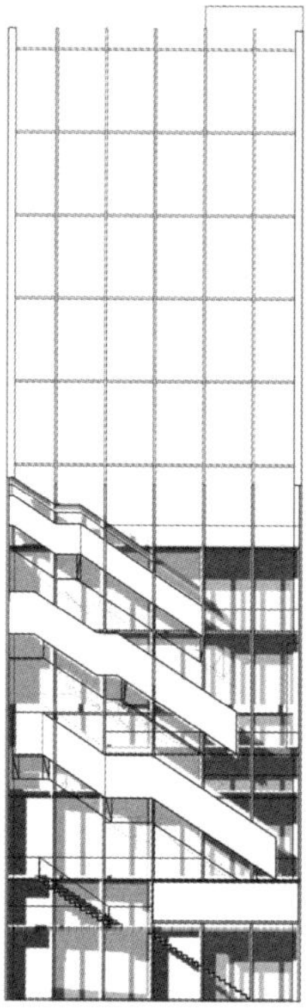

125TH STREET
NORTH ELEVATION

125TH STREET
SOUTH ELEVATION

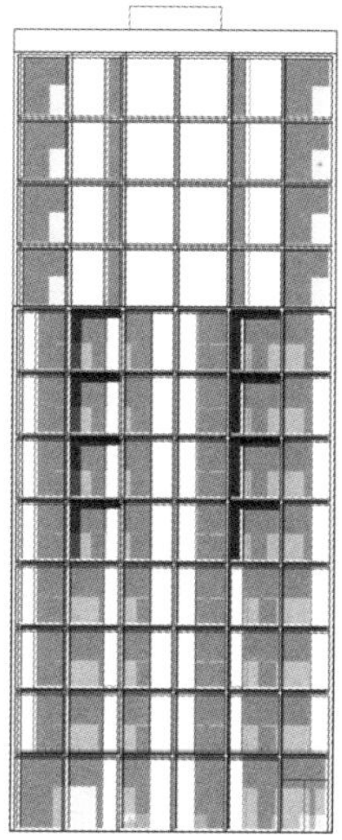

124TH STREET
SOUTH ELEVATION

124TH STREET
NORTH ELEVATION

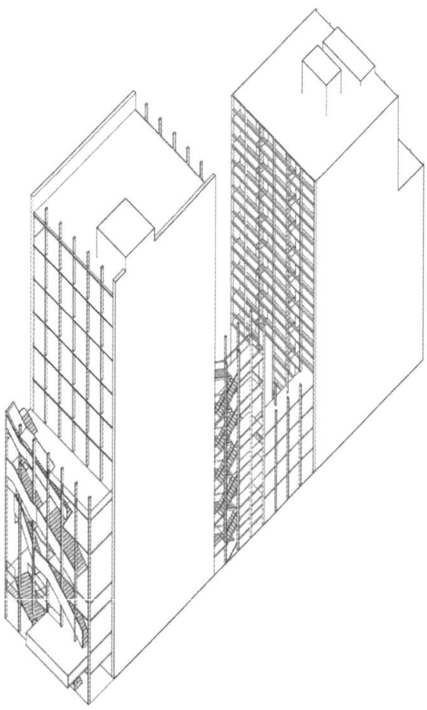

OPPOSITE TOP Elevations

OPPOSITE BOTTOM Axonometric view from 125th Street

ABOVE Interaction of building and urban life on 125th Street

ABOVE Residential unit

OPPOSITE Looking at the courtyard

Katherine Stege
Cultural Network

Equal parts affordable housing and digital-arts community building, Harlem's Mart 125 is a mixed-use through-block structure that deals with the strict programmatic, economic, and urban demands of the developer while addressing the nuanced cultural context of contemporary Harlem. This project proposal interprets the building's role as a network of cultural production and display, ranging from the urban to the individual scales, focused around ideas of identity, layers of control, and programmatic performance. Using formal and material choices related to the nature of the site and the climate, the building is constructed with an inward-focused scheme woven together through a transitional middle. The flexibility of various spaces, especially at the urban level, allows for continuous occupation and connectivity.

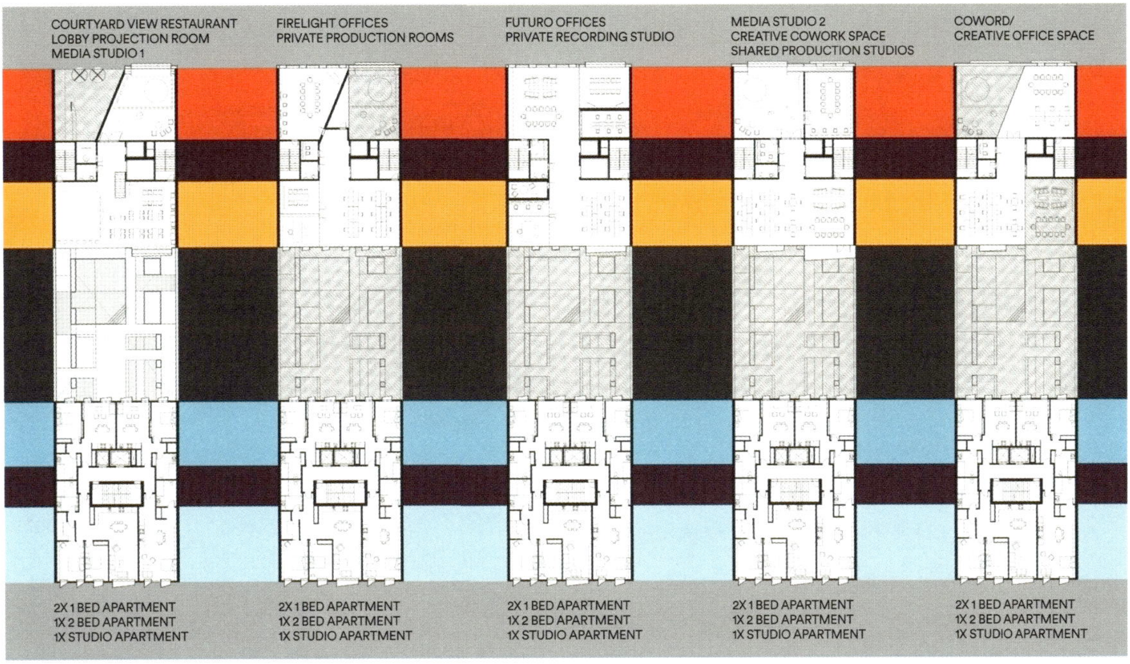

TOP Plans of all levels zoned by use and circulation

BOTTOM Section from 124th Street looking west

Section from 125th Street looking east

Elevation on 124th Street

ABOVE Window surrounds determined by sun angles

OVERLEAF Rendering of residential courtyard

Vincent Chang, Principal at Grimshaw, in conversation with curator and writer Vladimir Belogolovsky

Vladimir Belogolovsky How do you feel about your experience on the studio jury, and how would you define the goals and intentions of the studio?

Vincent Chang The studio provided students with the nearly real-life experience of working on a project that is actually being built in the city. They were very successful at addressing a complex program and resolving a multitude of issues, from broader planning concerns to navigating the interests of many different stakeholders. Many projects were truly remarkable, with images that were precise yet suggestive and exploratory.

VB What did you focus on in your discussion of the student projects?

VC Ultimately I was looking for the stories behind each project and for what a day in the life of the building might actually feel like. The number of apartments and the square-footage of retail space or what have you, all of these details are a list of possibilities. It is up to the architect to imagine the experiential qualities to project forward. It was rewarding to witness the level of passion with which the students presented their ideas. It was evident that they felt a very strong and personal relationship not just with

ABOVE View from the solar-shaded window of a musician's home facing south by Katherine Stege

OPPOSITE Stacked spatial diagram of restaurant by Kirk Henderson

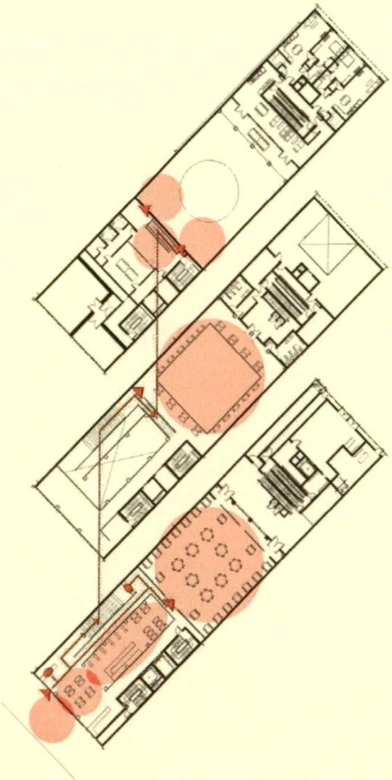 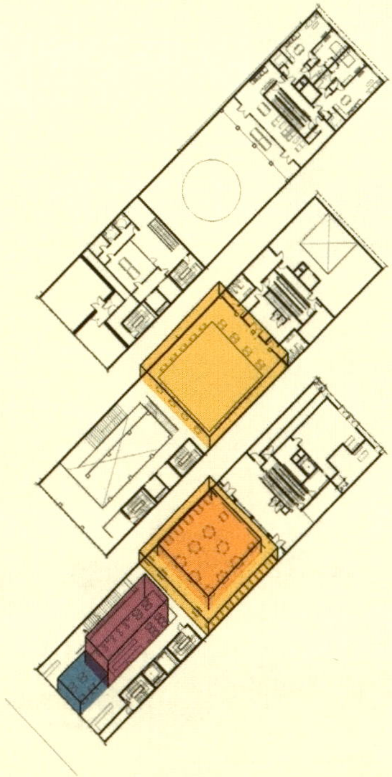

the site but also with the place and its culture. The students applied a great amount of imagination to considering everything from planning constraints to structuring journeys through the buildings as means for creating socially relevant and cohesive spaces.

VB The students' solutions for the building envelopes were quite similar, which indicates that there were set boundaries that none of the proposals attempted to challenge in any substantial way.

VC Precisely. That speaks to the fact that the goal of the studio was to have the students address a situation that is as close to reality as possible. Initially they worked as a group to explore the zoning opportunities, so they all started from a good understanding of how these very real requirements would shape the design potential. Despite the very precise site and zoning constraints, the students demonstrated phenomenal creative diversity in design solutions for elements such as programs, layouts, and meeting points.

VB Would you say these projects could be confused with some of those being developed in the city today?

VC I think many of them could be built, and the developers could learn from them.

VB What would be the biggest challenge for developers in realizing these projects?

ABOVE Cultural uses along 125th Street in a project by James Kehl.

OPPOSITE Vincent Chang, in cap, listens to student, Eunil Cho, presentation at final jury.

VC The biggest challenge would be to refrain from aiming at a particular, immediate agenda and take a long-term, more holistic view of the project in the context of the neighborhood as well as promote alignment among the broadest range of stakeholders. The projects we discussed were inclusive, engaging, and deliberately complex. They emphasized the interaction and multiplicity of complex forces present in a heterogeneous city like New York, addressing the real cultural needs of the place. It can be a challenge for developers to recognize and promote that in line with commercial interests.

VB There were a great deal of nuances that required closer examination, but judging purely based on first impression, the project envelopes looked like different options designed by the same team.

VC I didn't have this impression. I think they were immensely creative given the very tight margins within which they had to play. Certainly you didn't get one form that was entirely different from the next. The conditions the students operated under were such that they really had to fight for every inch and understand how to maximize any opportunities they had. The success of the studio was in the fact that the best projects were very believable as places you'd want to be.

VB Jonathan Rose stated that his mission is to repair the fabric of cities, towns, and communities while preserving the surrounding land. What do you believe is the developer's role?

VC He says it beautifully, and it would be great if there were more developers like him. When you work with him as a client you come away with the feeling that you are constantly being challenged in a very thoughtful way. The truth is that we need cities; they are our greatest inventions and assets for a sustainable future. They train us to be good citizens and make them places where we can exchange ideas easily and freely. All of us—city planners,

developers, and architects—should be responsible for making good buildings that will last a long time and have positive impacts on the communities they serve. Of course New York can lack sentimentality, which is what also drives its energy. Change is important for every major city, but it does not have to be preceded by destruction. The High Line is a good example of that. What was great about the Bass Studio is that it pushed the students to create programs that would project local interests to ensure connections between people and places.

VB What do you imagine as the ideal partnership between a professor and a student?

VC A professor should try to create circumstances in which a student can do his or her very best work. And the student, in this dynamic, is responsible for challenging the terms within which the professor might have framed the opportunities. Ultimately it is about mutual trust and dialogue, and I think this studio achieved that. The professors created the right environment and conditions for exploration and enquiry on the part of the students. I think they knew when to turn their own volume down in order to listen and engage the students. This experience was a great lesson for me in how to conduct a creative dialogue.

Xinyi Wang
New Marketplace

The purpose of this project's design is to create a place in Harlem that bridges past, present, and future while focusing on the street culture, community, and media sector. The program is focused on bringing together different functions in one common venue, the 24/7 F&B concourse, at street grade. A connection to public facilities and community spaces is emphasized with a grand opening and mini plaza created by a street-wall setback. The site includes a base with a yard and two towers to maximize the full extent of the zoning envelope.

The residential tower designed for retired jazz musicians receives sunlight from the 124th Street orientation and has views onto the shared backyard. The office tower has generous ceiling height and flexible sunlit rooms on the south. Several art pieces inspired by Harlem culture and history are incorporated into the architecture, including a mural and tiles in the restaurant, and a sculpture installed on the top floor of the office tower.

Harlem
soul house
bar & kitchen
NYC
GAP
Factory Store

RESIDENTIAL ENTRANCE
124TH ELEVATION

COMMUNITY FRONT
COURTYARD ELEVATION

CULTURAL FRONT
COURTYARD ELEVATION

CULTURAL ENTRANCE
125TH ELEVATION

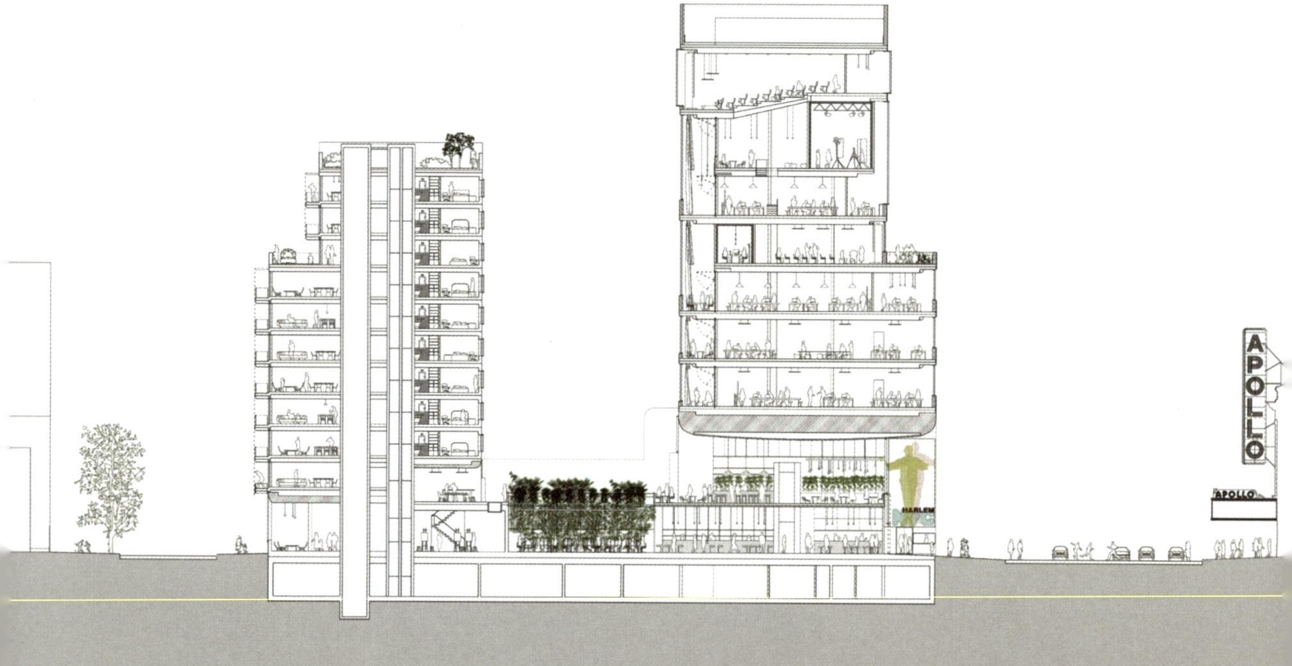

SECTION 1' = 1/8' 0"

PREVIOUS PAGE View from 125th Street

OPPOSITE TOP Elevations

OPPOSITE BOTTOM Section looking west

ABOVE View of courtyard

View of restaurant

Closing Comments

Students in conversation with Sara Caples, Everardo Jefferson, and Jonathan Rose

Synopsis

After completing the Bass Studio, the students and professors met at the Midtown Manhattan office of developer Jonathan Rose, on the twenty-third floor of the landmarked Fred F. French Building. Sara Caples initiated the discussion with an overview of the studio's mission and then asked for opinions on how successful the studio was in introducing the constraints students will encounter in the "real world" after they enter the workforce.

Three dominant themes emerged: the developer's process and constraints on design, a move away from purely formalistic concerns, and the uncertainties (and opportunities) inherent in working directly with clients. In general the studio served as early career exposure to designing outside of the abstract academic context, with cause-and-effect considerations taking center stage in the students' observations, reflections, and analyses.

Participants

JR Jonathan Rose
SC Sara Caples
EJ Everardo Jefferson
EC Eunil Cho
JE Jessica Elliott
DF Dov Feinmesser
JK James Kehl
JEK Jenny Eunhyung Kim
JP Jeannette Penniman
XW Xinyi Wang
CT Colette Taber

"Vision-reality Constraints" and Channeling the Client's Perspective

For many of the students the appeal of the studio was learning about the development process, which meant embracing "real-world project constraints." Jonathan Rose spoke about facilitating a "nonstatic studio" by introducing ideas capable of "informing" students throughout their careers. Rose coined the term "vision-reality constraints," which he described as not so much about form as about "making the program live." Caples repeated this sentiment later in the discussion, referring to "different paths" that can be taken after an architect understands a project's basic constraints, when he or she is free to develop alternate ideas.

EC Learning about the developer's point of view was an introduction to the client perspective too. This relationship is significantly more difficult to develop while working in a huge

ABOVE From left to right: James Kehl, Katherine Stege, Sara Caples, Dov Feinmesser, Everardo Jefferson, Kirk Henderson, and Jeannette Penniman at the Pathe Foundation. Paris, France

ABOVE From left to right: Dov Feinmesser, Jessica Elliott, and Xinyi Wang. Le Corbusier, Villa La Roche, Paris, France

OPPOSITE From left to right: Katherine Stege and Kirk Henderson. Le Fondation Cartier, Paris, France

office. We have minimal opportunities to think like a developer and, similarly, to recap project ideas and advantages. So we listen in and practice thinking like developers.

DF Although the project involved cultural and residential components, we pivoted away from the housing for the first half of the semester. We found it difficult to address both programs at once and dive deep. Maybe the solution is to work in pairs.

JEK The studio project felt at times like an exercise in trying new things. I would have liked to see more numbers upfront, in addition to the pro forma, to prevent the effort from becoming too abstract.

JK Access to the pro forma came too late in the project. In addition to the financial breakdown, we needed the reasoning behind the numbers so that we could understand them as the owner does.

JE It is possible to latch onto constraints in order to choose design over project limitations, although this approach may not be for everyone.

EC My goal now is to learn how to think like a developer. There's the potential to make better buildings if I can do a better job of convincing others of a design's merits from the perspective of a developer. Perhaps assuming the role of a developer when practicing architecture is the way to go.

JP I think it's possible to make a design according to your own priorities, but you have to be able to defend those choices in terms of functionality. The objective is to achieve some balance and to realize the project, which requires focusing on what the client sees as important.

Formalism versus Design Constraints

The students spoke of a tension in school between the application of formal tools and severe economic constraints on design. Much of the gravity of this dynamic waned once they entered the workforce and it was replaced by a new set of challenges.

Remarking on how the studio project involved analyzing and responding to an evolving African-American cultural context, Rose noted: "Neighborhood politics reflect memories, in addition to what the community is becoming. Because Harlem is vastly in transition, you had to confront both the politics and the reality." The extent to which the building would reflect each aspect was an individual choice.

EJ Is an abstract architectural language better equipped to tackle these types of consideration? Is it valuable for grappling with a difficult artistic journey?

JP Discussions about what the shapes of things should be have been replaced by asking how we can make the building distinctive. We have been released from focusing exclusively on form; much of our attention is now shifted to the multitude of project elements affecting how a building is realized.

DF The studio helped prepare me for the inevitable back-and-forth conversations about constraints to the building's design versus what we want to achieve. In response to feedback from the owner, developer, and consultants, we adjust, mold, and even reconsider the vision to work within the current restrictions placed before us.

JK Engagement efforts, whether about site considerations (What is "special" about the site?) or specific cultural attributes, can be about trying to fit into an architectural tradition.

JP Decisions have consequences when you are considering, for example, the curtain wall or ceiling height. To grapple with these issues is both exciting and frustrating. We can't make form from pure design, just as we can't propose solutions without thinking about the consequences of design choices.

DF A school project solution can revolve around design. In contrast, professional practice demands that we also consider other project elements.

JEK Responding conceptually to a cultural landmark is not necessarily about avoiding the easy criticism. Because of Harlem's changing demographics, there is no exclusive architectural connection.

JP We wanted to go beyond the aesthetic ornament of Harlem and enter

into an artistic exercise where we could submerge ourselves in the culture and address discrete challenges clarified through exploration. Some of these challenges could be solved with formalistic tools, but not without artistic or expressive risk.

XW The formal tools available to us have limitations. Trained as architects, we don't necessarily know how to ask a client what they think is right. "Fact-based questioning" tools helped with the compressed studio schedule but were less effective for gauging a community's attitude. For example, a place may have a history as a neighborhood marketplace, but to rebuild requires working within current financial realities.

EC We're not just making stuff; we're in the thinking business.

ABOVE LEFT From left to right: Sara Caples, Everardo Jefferson, Jeannette Penniman, James Kehl, Katherine Stege, Xinyi Wang, Kirk Henderson, Eunil Cho, Jessica Elliot. Palais de Tokyo, Paris, France

ABOVE RIGHT Melody Song. Centre Pompidou, Paris, France

Shadow on the sidewalk at Caples Jefferson Architects' Weeksville Heritage Center, 2013.

JP Buildings are complicated. Different parts of a building have to be addressed at different stages and as spaces are prioritized. But even the back-burner spaces have their moments. You can't design everything at once or you will be overwhelmed.

The Uncertainty of the People Factor

Although the studio provided the students with numerous opportunities to work in a collaborative team environment—researching in groups, for example—professional practice has proven even less conducive to independent designing. Referencing the client's programmatic agenda, Everardo Jefferson challenged the students to consider the "push and pull" of competing interests as potential inspiration for design solutions. As Rose advised, "First consider the client's needs and how and/or why they might have arrived at these [conclusions]. And only then open up the discussion to alternatives."

DF Perhaps the most pronounced difference between school and real-life practice is that we now know what questions the client might ask. The studio encouraged us to prepare ourselves prior to coming to the table, including being ready with information about costs, regulations, and code. If you want to be treated like you know what you are talking about, you need to be prepared for these factors.

JE The studio presented us with the professors' particular viewpoints. Jonathan Rose has a long history with affordable housing, and Caples Jefferson Architects works with underserved communities. It's personal.

JK I wish we had had more direct engagement with the Harlem community. There are always at least two sides to approaching a design. How can we connect to the urbanism and street-level activity, and how can we capture the aesthetic of Harlem? How do both of these big ideas translate into details?

JEK Although Harlem was essentially a local studio subject, and I appreciated being able to walk the neighborhood, I still felt "displaced."

DF Remember there are always things going on simultaneously, as well as the division of labor to consider. So it was an ambitious project. There was value in what we wanted to achieve, but we were starting from scratch—no familiarity with Harlem and a limited understanding of the zoning issues. Perhaps with more time or provided with a base packet of zoning code analysis prior to the start of the studio, we could have achieved more.

JE Submitting a complete project scheme by midterm had its challenges, but an iterative design process was instrumental in quickly drafting and then discarding ideas. Multiple iterations had the benefit of pushing us forward to develop solutions that demonstrated the client's needs.

JP Presenting to the final jury allowed us to dive deeper into the details, which was a welcome switch in focus and felt like we were getting closer to what the client wanted.

Final Notes

Rose and several of the students acknowledged the limitations of academia. "Yale is not a trade school," Rose said, encouraging everyone to continue to "expand and explore" when presented with constraints. He added, "Compliant architecture is boring. The world wants you to do more."

Student Xinyi Wang described the studio as a "shortcut," which is an interesting choice of words for defining a transitional period as many of the students prepared to leave school and join a practice. In this context the studio served as a kind of bridge between having much taken care of and beginning the long process of building a professional portfolio over many years. The studio was intended to be an experience that could be referenced later and, ultimately, used to wash away perceived design constraints. Caples described the work of an architect as connected intrinsically to the "freedom to create space." As she said, "This was not meant to be only a planning exercise; it was intended to give the students more confidence in developing actual buildings."

Contributor Biographies

Sara Caples is principal and cofounder of Caples Jefferson Architects. Her early experience was focused on the design and direction of large projects, especially in the public realm. Since founding the firm in 1987 with Everardo Jefferson, she has remained committed to designing cultural, educational, and community centers for neighborhoods underserved by the design professions. Caples's architectural passions include detailed examination of program; marrying the brief to the real goals of the project; clear, open, and flowing space; editing the project design for architectural coherence; and use of color and materials that evoke specific cultural, and even emotional, responses. She is a frequent lecturer at schools as well as community and professional organizations. She has been a visiting professor at Syracuse University School of Architecture, City College of New York, University of Miami, and Yale School of Architecture.

Everardo Jefferson is principal and cofounder of Caples Jefferson Architects. An architect and industrial designer, his experience encompasses a broad range of skills including construction, project management, detailing, and the incorporation of design thinking at every level of development. His architectural passions include light, particularly the miracle of daylight and the many ways it can infuse space; the exploration of geometrical form, especially as it relates to the experience of place; strategic transparencies; persistent questioning of how materials and construction go together; and how the delight of construction can create fresh moments. Jefferson has served on the boards of social justice and educational institutions and taught at several architectural schools, most recently at Yale School of Architecture.

Jonathan F. P. Rose's business, public policy, and nonprofit work focuses on creating a more environmentally, socially, and economically responsible world. In 1989 he founded Jonathan Rose Companies, a multidisciplinary real estate development, planning, consulting, and investment firm. The company has completed $2.3 billion of transformational work in close collaboration with cities and nonprofits. He is a thought leader on a wide range of urban issues and the development of communities of opportunity. He has received MIT's Visionary Leadership Award and the Urban Land Institute's global award for excellence, among many other honors. Rose's book on how to create resilient cities, *The Well-Tempered City: What Modern Science, Ancient Civilizations,* and *Human Nature Teach Us About the Future of Urban Life*, was published by Harper Wave in 2016 and won the 2017 PROSE Award for outstanding scholarly work by a trade publisher. Rose is a trustee of Enterprise Community Partners and the Brooklyn Academy of Music, an honorary member of the American Institute of Architects, and honorary trustee of the American Museum of Natural History and Jazz at Lincoln Center. He plays bass and blues harp. Rose and his wife, Diana Calthorpe Rose, are the cofounders of the Garrison Institute, which connects inner transformation with outer solutions to relieve suffering in the fields of trauma, education, and the environment. Rose graduated from Yale University in 1974 with a BA in psychology and philosophy, and received a master's in regional planning from the University of Pennsylvania in 1980.

Colette Taber got her start as a business writer in the architectural community. She founded Word Munky Communications, a writing consultancy exploring where technical aspects of the built environment merge with how people live, work, and play. She has written for design practices in Philadelphia and New York City, including several legacy firms, AIA NYS Firm of the Year recipients, and AIA Fellows. The specialty consultants she works with represent the very best in their areas of expertise: architecture and interior design, planning and engineering, owner representation and project management, and open space design. Taber attended the University of Pennsylvania, with a BA in fine arts and English literature.

Vladimir Belogolovsky graduated from the Cooper Union school of architecture in 1996. He is founder of New York-based Curatorial Project, which focuses on curating and designing architectural exhibitions. Belogolovsky writes for *ArchDaily*, *Arquitectura Viva*, and *SPEECH*. His books include *Conversations with Peter Eisenman: The Evolution of Architectural Style* (DOM Publishers, 2016), *Conversations with Architects in the Age of Celebrity* (DOM Publishers, 2015), *Harry Seidler: LifeWork* (Rizzoli, 2014), and *Soviet Modernism: 1955-1985* (Izdatalstvo Tatlin, 2010). Belogolovsky has curated numerous exhibitions, including *Harry Seidler: Painting Toward Architecture* (touring since 2012); *Something Other Than a Narrative: Architects' Voices and Visions* (Mexico City, 2017); *Emilio Ambasz: Architecture Toward Nature* (Singapore, 2017); *Colombia: Transformed* (American tour, 2012–15); and *Chess Game*, Russian Pavilion, 11th Venice Architecture Biennale, 2008. Belogolovsky has lectured at universities and museums in more than thirty countries.

Robert A. M. Stern is a practicing architect, teacher, and writer as well as founder and senior partner of the internationally renowned design practice Robert A. M. Stern Architects. He was dean of the Yale School of Architecture from 1998 to 2016. Yale is also where he received his master's of architecture degree, in 1965. Prior to serving as dean at Yale, Stern was professor of architecture and director of the Historic Preservation Program at the Graduate School of Architecture, Planning, and Preservation at Columbia University. Stern initiated Yale's Bass Studio, where he shared his insights into academia's role in helping or hindering young architects as they prepare to ply their trade under real-world conditions.

Kenneth J. Knuckles is a distinguished attorney and public servant who resides in the Wakefield section of the Bronx. He has served as president and CEO of the Upper Manhattan Empowerment Zone (UMEZ) development corporation since January 2003. Under his leadership UMEZ has invested nearly $250 million in the economy of Upper Manhattan. Knuckles is a member of the NYC Planning Commission and was appointed vice chairman in February 2002 (and reappointed in 2011) by Mayor Michael R. Bloomberg. In 2011 he was appointed by governor Andrew M. Cuomo to the NYC Regional Economic Development Council and is a member of its executive committee. A graduate of the University of Michigan with a BS degree in architecture, Knuckles also holds a JD degree from Howard University School of Law.

Alexander Garvin has combined a career in urban planning and real estate with teaching, architectural practice, and public service. He is currently president and CEO of AGA Public Realm Strategists, a planning and design firm in New York that is responsible for initial master plans for the Atlanta BeltLine; Tessera, a new 700-acre community outside Austin, Texas; and Hinton Park, in Collierville, Tennessee. Between 1996 and 2005 he was managing director for planning at NYC2012, the committee established to bring the Summer Olympics to New York. As vice president for planning, design, and development for the Lower Manhattan Development Corporation, he was responsible for planning the rebuilding of the World Trade Center in 2002–03. Over the last forty-six years he has held prominent positions in five New York City administrations, including Deputy Commissioner of Housing and City Planning Commissioner. In addition to his professional work, Garvin has taught at Yale University, his alma mater, for the fifty years as adjunct professor of urban planning and management. He is the author of *The American City: What Works and What Doesn't*, now in its third edition; *The Planning Game*; *Public Parks: The Key to Livable Communities*; and *What Makes a Great City*.

R. Steven Lewis is an architect and a tireless advocate for social justice and diversity in the field of architecture. Currently he serves as the urban design director for the City of Detroit's Planning and Development Department, under director Maurice Cox. Previously he served as associate vice president of TRC's energy group. In January 2008 Lewis returned to Southern California to join Parsons Corporation as a design manager after working four years in the U.S. General Services Administration's Office of the Chief Architect, in Washington, D.C. He was a Loeb Fellow at the Harvard Graduate School of Design for the 2006–7 academic year. A founding partner of Los Angeles's RAW International in 1984, Lewis was an essential part of the firm's growth and success over the next twenty-four years. In December 2010 he concluded a two-year term as president of the National Organization of Minority Architects, traveling around the country to advocate for architects of color while cultivating diversity among the next generation of architects and designers. Lewis recently launched the consulting practice Thinking Leadership (TL), aimed at assisting clients in attaining superior outcomes through his engagement. More than anything, he is a facilitator of partnerships and alliances between groups and individuals who seek to use architecture and design to effect positive change in the world.

Vincent Chang is Grimshaw's group managing partner. Since 1996 he has played a key role in the practice's expansion and commitment to the quality, rigor, and reputation for excellence it is known for. He established the firm's New York office in 2001 and was instrumental in securing its AIA New York chapter's Medal of Honor Award in 2015. Chang has led many of the firm's most notable commissions in North America, including Via Verde—The Green Way, the winning entry in the "New Housing New York" competition, and Horno3: Museo del Acero, the adaptation of a historic blast furnace facility for the museum of steel in Monterrey, Mexico. He is a graduate of Cambridge University and a registered member of the Royal Institute of British Architects and the American Institute of Architects.

Image Credits

Otto Baits/ Esto/ p.42
Byron Company (New York, N.Y.)/ Museum of the City of New York. 41.420.378/ p.67
Cicada Design for Caples Jefferson Architects/ p.34, 38
Eunil Cho/ p.55, 85-89
Jessica Elliot/ p.72, 74, 91-95, 102, 127
Dov Feinmesser/ p.97-101
Getty images/ p.4-5
Sarah Gephart/ p.126
Edmund Vincent Gillon/ Museum of the City of New York. 2013.3.1.253/ p.68
William Gottlieb, William P. Gottlieb Collection, Music Division, Library of Congress/ p.125
Kirk Henderson/ p.79, 107-109, 151
John Jacobson/ p.29, 43, 47, 105, 127, 153
Jonathan Rose Companies/ p.18, 20-21, 23, 25, 27, 28
James Kehl/ p.48-51, 65, 70, 75, 110-117, 152
Jenny Kim/ p.59, 60, 119-123, 163-165, 167
Nick Lehoux/ p.35, 40-41, 168
Julian Olivas/ p.36-37
Jeanette Penniman/ p.104, 130-136
Steven Pisano/ p.73
Nina Rappaport/ p.2
Schomburg Center for Research in Black Culture Photographs and Prints Division, The New York Public Library. The New York Public Library Digital Collections, 1920. http://digitalcollections.nypl.org/items/510d47df-7943-a3d9-e040-e00a18064a99/ p.64, 66, 124
Melody Song/ p.53, 138-141
Katherine Stege/ p.6, 74, 76, 81, 127, 143-149, 150
Albert Vecerka/ Esto/ p.32, 33
Xinyi Wang/ p.103, 155-159